Walter Tetley
FOR CORN'S SAKE!

Walter Tetley

FOR CORN'S SAKE!

by Ben Ohmart

BearManor Media

2016

Walter Tetley: For Corn's Sake!

© 2016 Ben Ohmart

For information, address:

BearManor Media
P. O. Box 71426
Albany, GA 31708

bearmanormedia.com

Typesetting and layout by John Teehan

Published in the USA by BearManor Media

ISBN—1-59393-435-1
978-1-59393-435-4

Foreword

THERE ARE VERY FEW TODAY WHO REMEMBER the name of Walter Tetley. Some early TV fans may remember him as 'Sherman', the fresh-faced, bespectacled 'pet boy' of 'Peabody', a talking white beagle who also wore glasses and a red bow-tie, and lived in a penthouse. Peabody had invented the 'Way-Back Machine' in which this peculiar pair traveled through time and space, and got involved in all sorts of misadventures throughout history. It was an animated cartoon series that aired as a segment of the *Rocky and His Friends* TV show. Tetley supplied the voice for Sherman in all 91 episodes of *Peabody's Improbably History*.

Other older fans who can recall the golden age of radio should remember several of Tetley's other outstanding roles—as Leroy, the wise-cracking nephew of The Great Gildersleeve, and as the tough-talking delivery boy, Julius Abbruzio, on *The Phil Harris/Alice Faye Show*.

Early in his career Walter worked with Fred Allen who considered him an eminently skilled comedian to be reckoned with. He also worked on other highly rated radio comedy shows such as Jack Benny, George Burns and Gracie Allen, and Joe Penner. Walter skillfully played dramatic roles on classic shows such as *Cavalcade of America*, *Lux Radio Theater* and *Suspense*. He also had regular roles on continuing radio shows such as *Buck Rogers*. In addition, he gave voice to 'Tigger' on a radio version of *Winnie the Pooh*, as well as the role of 'Tip' in a serialization of *The Wizard of Oz*.

Tetley's radio career began in 1930 when he made weekly appearances on children's shows—*The Children's Hour* and *The Lady Next Door*—doing his remarkable impersonation of legendary Scottish entertainer, Sir Harry Lauder.

1

He gained renown for his precise comedy timing and sure-fire delivery, getting every possible nuance out of every line. Walter held his own while sharing the microphone with such show business legends as the Barrymores and Helen Hayes.

But very little is known of the actor's private life. It is recalled that he had the epitome of all stage mothers, who practically thrust him into the lucrative limelight. He magically managed to sound like a 12-year-old throughout his many years on radio and in voice-over work. He was a very private person and rarely granted interviews. Former co-workers recall his selfless nature and his utter lack of conceit.

Part of the mystery was unraveled when scrapbooks of his early career, that had been kept by his parents, were located. Also a wealth of information was found in a little black notebook that his father kept, listing each audition, broadcast and personal appearance that Walter made. These records provided much of the information found in these pages. You can read more about this in the closing chapter.

Memories fade and die, and if history is not passed on by the printed page, even the greatest personalities can be lost to the world. From Walter's scrapbooks and the little black notebook, I have pieced together as much of the story as possible. I located a few of the people Walter worked with, but there was little they could tell me. Only during the construction of the second edition of this book was I able to luck into some more personal information. If there is anyone out there who can possibly help fill in more gaps, please get in touch, and I'd be pleased to put out a third edition of this book.

Walter Tetley was a very big part of radio. I love him. If I could go back in time and meet *anyone*, it would be Walter.

He made us laugh and he must be remembered. Who can ever forget that voice?

Ben Ohmart
March, 2016

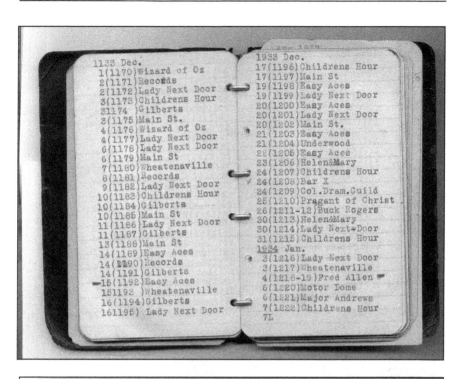

The little black notebook of radio credits, kept by Frederick Tetzloff.

I

ACCORDING TO ANGUS CAMPBELL, Walter Tetley's second cousin, once removed, "Walter's great grandfather (my great great grandfather) was the laird of a large 9,000 acre estate at Lochgair on the shores of Loch Fyne on the West coast of Scotland. Duncan MacIver Campbell was born Duncan Campbell Paterson in Kilrush, County Clare in Ireland around 1800 and came over to Scotland around 1840 after a family dispute with his father.

"Duncan was a tenant on the Lochgair estate and finally inherited it in 1853 along with the recognition of being head of the MacIver Campbell family, which can be traced back to the 12th century. Duncan had married an Irish woman, Elizabeth Russell, from Limerick in 1843 in London, but this marriage was a disaster from the start and did not last a year. His wife filed for divorce on the grounds of cruelty but she lost as it was proved she was not the victim of a physical assault and the courts did not recognize mental cruelty back then. Her family were rich Irish merchants and they supported her appeals to the Scottish Courts progressing as far as the House of Lords in London for the Law Lords to pronounce, but again Duncan prevailed.

"Following an affair with a servant, Duncan became the father of two daughters, Agnes and Flora (my great grandmother), and a son, Angus, Walter's grandfather. It was the baptism of Angus that finally earned Elizabeth her divorce, as the baptism proved adultery and a divorce was finally granted. Duncan went on to marry another Irish woman, a distant relative of his, in 1863. Both marriages failed to produce any legitimate children and Duncan's mistress/servant married a local village fisherman which produced another three children.

"Angus Campbell is shown on the 1861 Scottish census with his two Campbell sisters and three Fletcher step-siblings in a small fisherman's cottage in Lochgair, while his father was living the life of the local laird a mile away in the family Georgian Mansion. That said, Duncan seemed to give Angus every assistance in life, where his two sisters were left to their own devices, becoming house maids.

"We know from a letter Angus sent from New York back to a niece in Scotland, a daughter of Flora, who was coming to North America as a companion to a 'lady,' that Angus attended the Ball given at the nearby Inveraray Castle, ancestral home of the Dukes of Argyll to celebrate the marriage and homecoming of the Marquis of Lorn, son and heir of the Duke of Argyll. The Marquis, although heir to one of the largest estates in Scotland, and head of the mighty Clan Campbell, was still perceived as a commoner. But this marriage to Princess Louise, the daughter of Queen Victoria, was a very major event in Scottish history. In this letter Angus claims that the Marquis was a good friend and that on the evening of the Ball he danced with the Princess. Not bad for a 17 year old who only ten years previously was one of eight people in a fisherman's cottage.

"I know from census records, etc. that Angus went to University and became a writer, the Scottish term at the time for a Solicitor. This could only have been possible with the help and financial assistance of his birth father. Duncan died in 1881 and Angus married the following year and settled in Glasgow where they had three children in quick succession.

"From Court papers I know that Duncan died penniless. In fact he owed his son over £100, a large sum in those days. As he was illegitimate, Angus would never succeed his father to inherit the estate or position as head of the MacIver Campbell's. We can only speculate why he would uproot his young family in 1886 and emigrate for a life in New York. From New York census documents I know his addresses and occupation—he never worked as a Lawyer!

"This heritage, though, no doubt played a huge part in Walter's upbringing. His mother, Jessie, left Scotland when she was only two but she was obviously brought up a proud Scot and she would cling on to the family history of her grandfather and his lands and heritage rather than her housemaid grandmother!"

WALTER CAMPBELL TETZLOFF was born to Frederick Edward Tetzloff of New York and red-haired Jessie Campbell of Scotland on June 2, 1915. Frederick came to New York from Germany at an early age, while his mother was pure Scots with a strong passion for her homeland.

Until the height of Walter's radio career, when he then received his government pension, Frederick worked for thirty-five years in the

New York post office. Albert, Walter's older brother, and Jessie's sister Anna S. Campbell completed the early household. Albert married and moved into his own home in the 1930's.

The Tetzloffs lived at 128 Edwin Street in Ridgefield Park, New Jersey where Walter's mother urgently began carving out a career for her boy who had such natural talent. She was evolving into a stage mother and would often play Sir Harry Lauder records for her son to mimic, a trait which would serve him well in the coming years.

Vaudeville/music hall star Sir Harry Lauder (August 4, 1870 – February 26, 1950) was equally loved in the United States and in his homeland of Scotland, mainly due to his ability to mix his ethnic humor and songs with material that would be understandable to patrons of all backgrounds. He admitted, "If I came

Jessie Campbell Tetley was always proud of her Scottish ancestry.

to this county to just entertain a few Scots, it wouldn't pay me." Lauder had been knighted in 1919 for entertaining the troops in World War I, during which his son, an army captain, was killed.

Lauder was lauded by Presidents—he played golf with Warren G. Harding and met with Calvin Coolidge and Woodrow Wilson. On a tour of the United States one time, Theodore Roosevelt gave the actor the use of his private car. Sir Harry had a successful recording career which began in 1904 for Pathe, and he was making the incredible sum of $23,000 a week performing on the New York stage in 1912. It was to this stupendous fame that Walter Tetley linked himself at such an early age.

Walter at 1 year and 4 months old.

Young Walter in one of his first
photos in costume.

Walter Tetley, early 1930's.

In kindergarten at Lincoln School, Walter began singing songs at age five. Sometimes his teacher would request Scots songs from him when parents came to visit in order to show off her star pupil. Walter had picked up his mother's Highland accent, which he could turn on and off at will. His mother's friends, listening to wee Walter sing his heart out at home, persuaded Mrs. Tetzloff to dress the tiny boy in little Scots costumes and urged her to let Walter perform at a few local social events. His first public appearance was at a meeting of the Daughters of Scotia, to which Jessie belonged. Walter "wowed" them with his diminutive but enthusiastic impression of Sir Harry Lauder, one of Scotland's most popular entertainers, singing songs and telling jokes. Mrs. Tetzloff had made Walter a kilt and rented a miniature set of bagpipes for the event. The boy was a sensation.

Jessie, always eager for her boy to succeed, was active in many lodges and would add her son to the program of entertainments when there was a need for more talent for an upcoming fund raiser or charity event. And sometimes, even when there was not a need. Many of these early performances were given free of charge, but Mrs. Tetzloff was quickly becoming little Walter's agent and sought out more and better and *paying* venues for her child.

Two years later, when Walter was seven, Mrs. Tetzloff sent Walter out with a group of children on the vaudeville circuit with the Keith-Orpheum Company. They played throughout the East Coast where Walter developed his Wee Sir Harry Lauder routine more fully.

A vintage, unusual photo of young Tetley not in Scottish costume. Early 1930's.

It was around this time that Walter stopped growing. At the age of six or seven Walter's normal rate of development had been arrested by a glandular disorder. He did not pass through adolescence at the usual age and his voice did not change. The condition could have been from an imbalance of Thyroxin, a hormone produced by the thyroid gland, which results in stunted growth (and sometimes some degree of mental retardation) at an early age, but if Walter's condition was reviewed by a qualified doctor, it was not something saved among their family papers. If anything, it was a dark secret to be kept and used to its fullest advantage. As he grew in years only, Jessie cut Walter's age in half for promotional reasons, insisting the lad was still a child. No one seemed to question his blurred birth date too closely.

As early as November 1928 Walter was achieving notoriety with his talents. *The New York Times* pictured a youthful cast for an unknown revue, with little Walter decked up in Scottish garb, sitting center stage.

In late 1929 a family friend suggested to Mrs. Tetzloff that she should take Walter to NBC for an audition. By early 1930 Jessie felt that he was ready, having had the feedback of a lot of personal appearances to give her an objective view: Walter Tetley had talent. The proud mother billed him as Walter Campbell Tetley because she felt it sounded more Scottish.

On Saturday February 8, 1930 Walter auditioned for *The Children's Hour*. He was immediately booked to sing and give his Lauder impression on that series the following day. It was his first professional radio credit. To ensure that a proper list of credits was maintained, Walter's father began typing them in a little black, lined-paper notebook. He religiously

---

WALTER TETLEY

America's foremost Juvenile Scotch Entertainer, from the Children's Hour of Station W J Z, invites you to his party at the Floor Show at ———

WOODLAWN PARK

Sunday evening, August 2nd at 8:30 o'clock, when he will appear in person, together with five other high class act   Listen in on Sunday morning from 9 to 10 o'clock, then come out and meet   the evening. He also wants you to bring all the kiddies, as he is anxious to   them, too.

This Card will be accepted as one gate admission, when accompanied by a paid admission at 10 cents, on Sunday evening only, August 2nd.

Also, Just A Reminder — Saturday evening, August 1st, Gore's Kiddie Musical Revue of 25 Kiddies, on the Park stage.

kept it updated, listing not only titles of shows, but the correct order of performances, whether they were auditions, and which number show it was in Tetley's career.

The Children's Hour, later known as *Coast-To-Coast on a Bus* (and sometimes referred to as *The White Rabbit Line*), began on WJZ in New York in May of 1924. It introduced a good many child actors to the world, including Billy and Florence Halop, Bob Hastings, and of course little Tetley. The hour-long variety series was filled mostly with singing acts and became a 30 and 45 minute show after 1940, and continued until 1948 where it finally ended on ABC. The host was Milton Cross who "conducted" the bus on the White Rabbit Line, blowing his horn and introducing the various children and acts at stops along the way. Madge Tucker served as writer, producer and director, and also auditioned the children. It was one of Tetley's most enduring series in his pre-Gildersleeve years.

Six days after his radio debut Walter found himself on *The Barn Show*, another hour-long weekly children's program produced by Madge Tucker.

But the series that got Walter the most work of his early career was *The Lady Next Door*. Madge Tucker was again responsible for assembling the

Madge "The Lady Next Door" Tucker seated behind the figure of Krazy Kat, surrounded by many of the young actors she discovered. Walter is standing at far right, in pirate costume and false sideburns and mustache. Early 1930's.

Walter Tetley, center stage, in 1928.

talent. An article in the early 1930s claimed "she, it has become obvious, is deserving of the title of 'The Maker of Future Stars.' In her hands, to a great extent, rests the future of radio. The kids she is coaching and training are the celebrities of the next generation who will, by virtue of their early microphone education, be able to take care of the eventual requirements of radio broadcasting. Already her protégés are appearing individually on the Penner, Vallee and Cantor programs. You'll know most of them—little Nancy Kelly, Walter Tetley, Rosalyn Silver, the daughter in *The Goldbergs*, young Jim McCallion, and a flock of others."

Because of the success of *The Children's Hour* Madge began to write, direct and host the Monday through Friday *Lady Next Door*, on the NBC Red network. The sustaining fifteen-minute series began in 1929 and featured stories for children dramatized by her "neighborhood children," called "the Magic Circle." The cast included Florence Baker, Howard Merrill, Walter Tetley and many others. The series also had a brief life in early television. For Walter it was one of his most prolific credits, until the series ended in 1935.

After continuing the same weekly routine of radio jobs for a number of weeks, young Mr. Tetley was signed to a contract by the network and was hailed as the youngest male star under contract to NBC. In those hard times of the Depression he began to earn a weekly paycheck. The family moved into a larger, rented home in Edgewater, New Jersey and their surname was legally changed to Tetley.

The Lady Next Door, Madge Tucker, reads to some of her young protegés.
Walter sits on floor, left.

Walter, or more likely his ambitious mother-agent, continued to mix personal appearances with radio jobs. Possibly it was an attempt to fill in the odd gap when there was time off from radio. It also got his name out there more. In one of his earliest live performances, the "vest pocket edition of Harry Lauder" provided entertainment between the acts of Philip Barry's four-act comedy *White Wings*, directed by Miss Anne Fletcher Campbell, possibly a relation of Walter's, at Ridgefield School No. 2 in Ridgefield, New Jersey. It was sponsored by the Ridgefield Athletic Club. Walter's usual act consisted of Scottish songs and jokes in the Lauder vein.

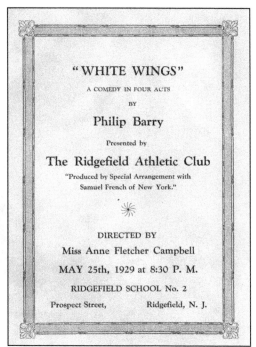

"WHITE WINGS"

A COMEDY IN FOUR ACTS

BY

Philip Barry

Presented by

The Ridgefield Athletic Club

"Produced by Special Arrangement with
Samuel French of New York."

DIRECTED BY

Miss Anne Fletcher Campbell

MAY 25th, 1929 at 8:30 P. M.

RIDGEFIELD SCHOOL No. 2

Prospect Street,   Ridgefield, N. J.

When Walter played the London Palladium in the early 1930s, the impressed manager told him, "What I like about you is you play to the gallery. And when you've got the gallery with you, you're all right."

The fact that Walter had no legitimate training for his success was all the more impressive. During later times, in the middle of his busy radio life, his mother wished he had had time to squeeze in some proper dramatic training. But Walter obviously needed no other instruction.

"Experience has been a better teacher for me than dramatic schools could be," the boy admitted. "I've heard kids practicing their recitations and it sounds like a lot of nonsense to me. They're learning to talk like radio announcers. When you interpret parts in a play for the radio, you're supposed to talk like people in the street. You learn that in the street, not in dramatic schools."

Continuing his personal appearances, Walter wowed 'em at the People's Palace in Jersey City, New Jersey on November 28, 1930. The 8:15 p.m. performance was a "Ladies' Night" in which Walter, called "a wee bit of Scotch," performed three songs: "The Waggle O' the Kilt," "When I was Twenty-One," and "Kiltie Lads." He followed "two rubes" by the name of Goodall and Lockwood.

The following month Walter and other specialty acts gave their time to help the poor and needy in Ridgefield Park, New Jersey with a performance given by the Elks of Ridgefield Park Lodge, No. 1506.

Secretary J.E. Williams gathered the talent and coordinated the December 17th show. A month later Walter received a thank you letter from Williams which began, "I know it's terribly late to tell you that you helped to feed 81 poor families at Christmas time and several before and since. That shoes and rubbers have been given to little kiddies and coal put in cellars." The social responsibility that Walter felt

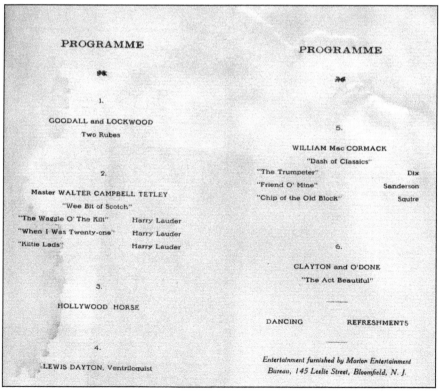

HAPMAN, EXALTED RULER   J. E. WILLIAMS, SECRETARY   A. J. KOENIG, TREASURER

Ridgefield Park Lodge, No. 1506

B. P. O. ELKS

RIDGEFIELD PARK, N. J.

January 23, 1931

Walter Tetley
Ridgefield Park, N. J.

Dear Friend:-

      I know it's terribly late to tell you
that you helped to feed eighty-one poor families at
Christmas time and several before and since. That
shoes and rubbers have been given to little kiddies
and coal put in cellars.

      Ridgefield Park Lodge of Elks passed a
resolution of thanks and appreciation December 17th and
every man arose enthusiastically to his feet and applauded
the fine work of those giving us the greatest show ever
in Bergen County.

      I had the honor to be the one to solicit the
talent and have charge of the entertainment. The work of getting together funds from the members and then the buying
and distribution of baskets also fell on me. My personal
business was almost neglected in December, but I got a thrill
out of it as I know you did in doing yours. Am just getting
up. Know you did'nt do your act for praise and will accept
this late day "Thank You" and know that 1506 does not forget.

Yours very truly,

J. Williams

Secretary

4 Mrs. Tetley is Walter's shrewd manager, has run his fees up over 600 percent. This picture was taken at their home Mother's Day

February
Sun. 9 (—1)
Sat. 15 (—2)
Sun. 16 (—3)
Sat. 22 (—5)
Sun. 23
Children's Hour
Barn Show
Children's Hour
Barn Show
Children's Hour

which Walter has appeared. This page from his notebook shows that Walter's first broadcast was Feb. 9, 1930, that he was on five times that week. Since then he's been on the air over 2821 times!

year, he invited "Uncle Jim" Harkins of "Town Hall Tonight" and Irene Rich over to christen it. She did the honor — but not with champagne. She used grape juice! The affair was aired over NBC

13 Walter wouldn't want it known, of course—but the day before this picture was taken he had a permanent! A movie contract demanded it!

14 Although he is only 17 years old, Walter earns $300 a week. In this he's unusual—but in every other respect he's a normal youth—like others, he wears no garters

12 To get to the radio studios in New York, Mrs. Tetley and Walter always take the ferry. Its dock is near by —and the fare is only a nickel. The crossing is at 125th Street. The tower of Riverside Church is seen in the background

15 In spite of the air-feud that Fred Allen & Walter carried on, they are very fond of one another. Walter is a very versatile actor. In addition to his stooge role, he can take any part given him, handle it perfectly—with little study!

11 His only piece of jewelry is a plain gold ring left him by a relative who was killed in the World War. The ring is still dented where the bullets found their mark

never left him. He always tried to do as much as he could with the talent he had.

Despite his spreading fame and accumulating fortune, Tetley remained unspoiled and unassuming. He always tried to avoid looking conspicuous. Other than an inexpensive wristwatch that his parents had given him, the only jewelry he wore was a ring that had been given to him by a relative who had been killed in World War I. The plain ring remained dented where a bullet had struck it.

II

IN 1930 SIR HARRY LAUDER HIMSELF saw Walter's famed impression of the Scottish star and was suitably impressed with the lad's skill. They had lunch together where Lauder was the first to call him "Wee Sir Harry Lauder." With official approval on his side, he began billing himself as just that.

The young man was still assembling a wealth of radio credits, of varying characters and supporting roles. Already giving interviews, Walter said at the time, "I had to imitate a baby bear on one program and an elf on the next. I've been elephants, calves, monkeys and a lot of other things." The February 1931 issue of *Radio Guide* did a feature on the "Babes in Radioland," showing Walter in his Scottish costume.

In the circle is Elizabeth Wragge, Betty of the *Red Davis* program; the lad in the Scotch costume is Walter Tetley, 12-year-old star who appears in youngster rôles on the Fred Allen program and others

Hoot, mon! 'Tis Walter Campbell Tetley himself! He's been singing in Scotland this summer and there he was called "NBC's Harry Lauder. Walter is now fourteen years old.

Wee Sir Harry Lauder

According to another radio magazine article (notorious for their sensational-sounding factual stories), on February 5, 1931, at three minutes to air time of the premiere episode of the 15-minute *Raising Junior* series, the boy who was to play Bobby still hadn't shown. Raymond Knight, collaborator and actor on the show was frantic when he grabbed hold of "nine"-year-old Walter stepping off the elevator. Rushing the kid up the stairs and into the studio, Knight pushed a script into his hand, caught his breath and proclaimed, "You're Bobby!" Tetley's unrehearsed performance was as smooth as a radio veteran's. He remained there six times a week for the next year. The show debuted on the NBC Blue network and was sponsored by Wheatina breakfast cereal, which later gave Walter a lot of work on *Wheatinaville*, a daily quarter-hour serial on NBC, also known as *Billy Bachelor*, about the editor of a newspaper who had twin nephews, Peter and Pan.

Another report told that Walter had come to the *Raising Junior* audition with a friend who got the part. Tetley didn't even try out for it. But the next day, after he had finished an episode of *The Lady Next Door*, he calmly walked out of the elevator when that same frantic hand grabbed

Stars of *The Lady Next Door*, Audrey Egan and Walter Tetley, share
a soda in the early 1930's.

him for the live *Raising Junior* broadcast. This report put his subsequent run as a regular at four years.

Regardless, there was no holding him—or his manager mother. Through the early 1930s his radio appearances racked up at an incredible rate, sometimes as many as five different shows a day. The little black notebook recorded shows such as *Uncle Abe & David*, a quarter-hour series starring Parker Fennelly and Arthur Allen; *The Coo Coo Hour*, actually *The Cuckoo Hour*, a quarter-hour variety show; and *Eno*, really *The Eno Crime Club*, "another action-packed radio riddle—giving you a chance to play detective yourself. Listen carefully so you can solve the puzzle from the clues in tonight's episode." This series, presented in both quarter and half-hour formats featured the main character "Spencer Dean," a famous private eye known as "The Manhunter."

Other series included: *Emerald Isle*, a children's adventure series; *Big Time Radio Household* (noted in the black notebook as simply *Household*), a variety show on which Walter presented his Wee Sir Harry Lauder impersonation; *Friendship Town*, a variety series on WJZ; and *The Adventures of Helen & Mary*, presenting children's stories, predating *Let's Pretend*. Along with all these new shows Walter kept busy with his regular series, and enough auditions to prove his demand was high. More often than not, a day or two after an audition, Walter would find himself on a new series.

He performed his "Wee Sir Harry" act more than several times on radio, gaining enough media attention to herald several glowing reviews of the act. Entertaining at the Junior Mechanics' Dinner in Lackawanna, Pennsylvania Walter "took the audience and thousands of listeners in by storm. This young lad, twelve years of age, gave imitations of Harry Lauder in songs and sayings that kept his hearers in hearty laughter. His pleasing personality, with a smile that can't wear off, and his various gestures mystified the audience and left an impression that will long be remembered."

Local political and civic leaders who attended the tribute to America's two outstanding statesmen at the Washington-Lincoln banquet in the Hotel Jermyn were equally impressed with the live act.

With the accompaniment of Helen Taylor at the piano, Walter performed his wee songs for the benefit of the 28th Floral Chapter of the Order of the Eastern Star at Pythian Temple on 135 West 70th Street in New York City on January 10, 1931.

He again did his "specialty act" for the Rotary Club of Yonkers' fourth annual Minstrel Show on Wednesday evening, March 11, 1931.

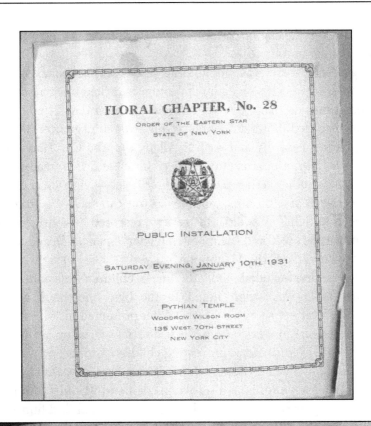

FLORAL CHAPTER, No. 28

ORDER OF THE EASTERN STAR
STATE OF NEW YORK

PUBLIC INSTALLATION

SATURDAY EVENING, JANUARY 10TH. 1931

PYTHIAN TEMPLE
WOODROW WILSON ROOM
135 WEST 70TH STREET
NEW YORK CITY

New York, January 2nd, 1931.

...rs and Brothers:

The 224th stated meeting of Floral Chapter No. 28, O. E. S.,
...ld in the Woodrow Wilson Room, Pythian Temple, 135 West
...t, New York City, on Saturday evening, January 10th, 1931.
...clock.

OPENING CEREMONIES

...EPTION TO THE WORTHY MATRON AND OFFICERS
...Y THE WORTHY PATRON ALEXANDER CREEKMORE

"Onward Christian Soldiers"
Margaret Seymour, Worthy Matron

INSTALLATION CEREMONIES

WORTHY WILLIAM W. GRAHAM
Installing Officer
assisted by:

...rgaret Seymour .... Grand Marshal
...xander Creekmore .... Assistant Grand Marshal
...p Harriet C. Meyer, P.D.D. .... Grand Chaplain

PROGRAM

.... By Arthur Clough, Tenor
Accompanied by Cora Sardo

...NS .... By Walter Campbell Tetley

"Wee" Sir Harry Lauder
Accompanied by Helen Taylor
By special arrangements with the National Broadcasting Company

.... By Julia Lehman
Accompanied by Helen Taylor

.... By Arthur Clough, Tenor
Accompanied by Cora Sardo

...NS .... By Walter Campbell Tetley
Accompanied by Helen Taylor

OFFICERS TO BE INSTALLED
FOR 1931

MRS. MAY BARSNESS	Worthy Matron
MR. CHARLES E. MILLER	Worthy Patron
MRS. ELIZABETH CREEKMORE	Associate Matron
MRS. BLANCHE BRUZIE	Treasurer Emeritus
R. W. JENNIE WILSON, P. G. R.	Treasurer
R. W. ANNIE H. FINCH	Secretary
MRS. NORMA BEAUX HOYT	Conductress
MRS. LETITIA PETETIN	Associate Conductress
W. MARGARET SEYMOUR	Chaplain
MISS MILDRED BAUER	Color Bearer
MRS. ELDA S. MILLER	Marshal
MRS. M. S. BEATH	Associate Matron
MRS. LUCY C. JACOBS	Historian
MRS. CORA SARDO	Organist
MISS JULIA LEHMAN	Warder
R. W. FRANK DE VALLE	Sentinel
MISS MADELINE GENARD	Adah
MRS. ELIZABETH COOK	Ruth
MRS. HELEN KLITTER	Esther
MRS. EDITH OSTERHAUT	Martha
MRS. MARIAN CHAMBERLIN	Electa
R. W. WILLIAM FINCH, P.G.C.	Trustee

HOSTESS

R.W. HARRIETT C. MEYER, P.D.D.G.M.

AND

FLORAL STAFF

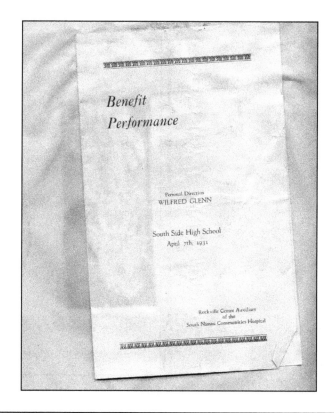

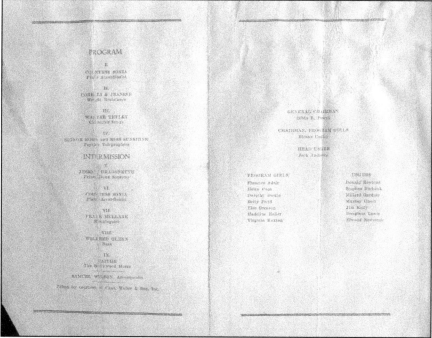

THE ROTARY CLUB
OF YONKERS
Samuel Hayward, *President*

FOURTH ANNUAL
MINSTREL SHOW

WEDNESDAY EVENING, MARCH 11, 1931
EIGHT-FIFTEEN O'CLOCK
NATHANIEL HAWTHORNE JUNIOR HIGH SCHOOL

Greetings

The Rotary Club of Yonkers extends a cordial welcome to its friends in appreciation of the support given this presentation of their Fourth Annual Minstrel.

The entertainment represents our sincere endeavor to make the evening an enjoyable one for you and also helps us to raise the funds for our Boys' Work. Your patronage insures the success of the Boys' Work Committee in financing our summer camp activities for the underprivileged boys of this city.

The measure of your pleasure bespeaks our success.

ROTARY THANKS YOU

—o—

Program

OVERTURE—*"Faust"*	Craven's Orchestra
OPENING CHORUS	Entire Company
SOLO—*"Ah, Sweet Mystery of Life"*	Werner G. Klebe
END SONG—*"You're Driving Me Crazy"*	Arthur Witte
SPECIALTY	Walter Tetley
END SONG—*"It Takes a Long, Tall Brown Skin Gal"*	Ed Spitz
SAXOPHONE SOLO	Alvin Weisfeldt
SPECIALTY	Sally Wilson
END SONG—*"Hello Beautiful"*	Harold Garrity
SONG AND DANCE SPECIALTY	Thelma Hassett's Pupils
SOLO—*"Friend of Mine"*	Norman Jolliffe
END SONG—*"Ninety-nine Out of a Hundred"*	Jud McCarthy
CLOSING CHORUS	Entire Company

—o—

Grateful acknowledgement is made to Thelma Hassett for the Girl Dancing Specialty; Harry Daniels for Lithographs.

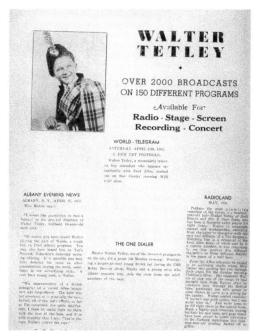

The completely musical night took place at the Nathaniel Hawthorne Junior High School.

Tetley may have been becoming a national radio star, but his mother realized the significance of public performances, and giving something back to the community. That moral sense was obviously highly ingrained in Walter at an early age.

On April 7, 1931 he appeared in a benefit performance for South Side High School in New Jersey for the Rockville Centre Auxiliary of the South Nassau Communities Hospital. He was third on the bill, after a piano accordionist and a "weight resistance" duo, and again performed character songs.

On May 1st he appeared at Pottstown Band's May Festival of Music, "featuring boy artists from *The Children's Hour* of Station WJZ." At 8:30 p.m. in the Victor Theatre a musical evening ensued, led by conductor William F. Lamb, who also played cornet and marimba.

Tetley appeared at Stevens Memorial Hall "under the management of NBC Artists Service" on May 14, 1931. He was hailed as "the star performer in the Clan MacLennan concert" to journalists. He even appeared at the fourth birthday party of the Edgewater Chapter O.E.S. in a parish house.

He was usually managed by Frances Rockefeller King of the Private Entertainment Department of the National Broadcasting Company, and

A wee bit of Scotland, circa 1932.

later on by NBC Artists Service, George Engles, managing director. NBC was aggressively marketing their little star; they knew it would only help their shows, too. The headline of one ad instructed event leaders that they could have "a wee bit of Scotch for your next show" and pressed the point home that a child star was cheaper than a full-grown one: "Enjoy big entertainment by a small star at a small price. This thirteen-year-old radio star is a thrifty buy. A rare comedian who will brighten any entertainment and has a repertoire as extensive as most adult performers." It was a campaign that continued to pay off, for star and studio both.

RADIOLOG

What's On The Air

5c
Per Copy

WEEK OF JULY 26, 1931

Walter Campbell Tetley—Juvenile Star
(Story on Page 21)

To some at NBC he was known as "Peanuts." But his fan mail kept growing at a remarkable rate, mostly from kids of his own age.

For all his hard work Walter was rewarded with his face on one of his few magazine covers for the week of July 26, 1931. His famous winking, smiling photograph lit up the five cents issue of *Radiolog*.

From June 27 to June 30, 1931 Walter (usually credited "of *The Lady Next Door and The Children's Hour*") appeared in a review with

Billy De Wolfe, the Kurto Trio, Joe and Jane McKenna ("in Mirth and Melody"), and others. Not much detail is known about most of his public appearances except for ads and small articles saved in the two scrapbooks which the family were beginning to keep. Even four-day events such as this received surprisingly little press.

But it was all beginning to pay off. Some of the news items that appeared in the press began to hint that Tetley was "a natural for motion

Walter and kids in an unknown review, early 1930's.

pictures." When it reached Jessie's ears she wanted to be certain that when the opportunity presented itself, he would be ready and waiting. She arranged for him to have voice and acting training at Hugh McClarin's studio in Ridgefield. But Hollywood would have to wait a few years.

In November of 1931 Walter was performing "in aid of the maintenance fund for the new home of the Children's Shelter of Manhattan" at the Selwyn Theatre on 235 West 113th Street. Aiding children in need was something he would continue to do for the rest of his life. In this case, young "Walter Campbell Tetley (courtesy National Broadcasting Company)" was joined by a host of luminaries. Lillian Roth, Sophie Tucker, and Thelma White were just a few of the film, radio and stage names that took part.

Another benefit show around this time began at midnight, at the Loew's Theatre in Jersey City on Thanksgiving, 1931. Robert L. "Believe It Or Not" Ripley, Ray Bolger, Ed Sullivan, Helen Kane and at least twenty other acts joined Walter for the ambitious production which benefited National Motion Picture Week for Local Unemployment Relief, sponsored by Mayor Frank Hague. On the following December 2nd Walter received a letter of thanks at his 740 Riverside Drive residence in New York City:

"Words are puny things when one attempts to express gratitude for such kind cooperation as you recently gave us. It was splendid, and I know all Jersey City would tell you the same thing, were it able to make itself heard.

"It was a source of great satisfaction to all of us and I am sure it will be to you, when I tell you the police report that twenty-five hundred persons were turned away from the theatre. Incidentally, our show at Loew's Jersey City was the only one in the city that played to capacity house.

"I hope that we did not cause you to lose too much sleep and rest assured that I feel so deeply obligated to you that I won't impose upon your good nature again for a long time.

"With every good wish for your future success, I am

"Sincerely yours,

"S. Jay"

A letter from Mayor Frank Hague also came before Christmas, ending with "the entertainment was delightful and the financial returns exceeded our highest expectations."

FRANK HAGUE

December 3, 1931.

Dear Mr. Tetley:

May I hope that word of my appreciation for the prompt response and generous aid you gave our Midnight Shows for the unemployed on Thanksgiving Eve may be a slight recompense for the substantial and unselfish contribution you made to their success?

The entertainment was delightful and the financial returns exceeded our highest expectations.

Thanking you again, believe me,

Sincerely,

Frank Hague
M a y o r.

Mr. Walter Campbell Tetley,
740 Riverside Drive,
New York City.

III

IT'S BEEN SAID THAT BY THE TIME WALTER was sixteen (1931) he had made 3,250 radio appearances. Most of these shows no longer exist. Some credits recorded in the little black notebook only gave the name "Records," which more than likely meant transcription discs recorded for later broadcast. Unfortunately, Walter's parents did not indicate what these "Records" were, shrouding his credit list in further mystery.

On March 11, 1931 NBC released a press statement proclaiming their little star had had his contract renewed for two more years.

He traveled extensively in the Eastern states between radio dates. Pottstown, Pennsylvania, Yonkers, New York, Scranton, Pennsylvania, Trenton, New Jersey, Washington, D.C., and many other theatres and civic clubs were just a train journey away.

At a Sunday school picnic in Allentown, Pennsylvania's Central Park on July 16, 1931 Walter appeared and sang several of his most popular numbers. "You'll like him and his Scotch songs," one advance publicity paper heralded. "Don't forget the date. We want the biggest turnout we've ever had." Another newspaper item wrote that Picnic Committee Chairman Mr. Walp met with Walter weeks before at WJZ studios and found the young lad to be "astoundingly bright for a boy of not quite fourteen years of age" and "that he has remained entirely unspoiled and wholesome despite the fact that he has received national recognition for his talent." A leaflet which was handed liberally around proclaimed, "The fourteen-year-old entertainer, well known on *The Children's Hour* from WJZ, will be with us in person, dressed in his Kilts, etc. You will have him with you all day and evening. This charming little fellow will sing for you both afternoon and evening. Paul Held will be his accompanist." FREE MILK, ICE CREAM, LOLLY POPS, GAMES, CONTESTS, SPECIALTIES!

Around this time the Tetleys moved to 13 Adelaide Place in Edgewater, New Jersey. They rented the small seven-room house (and roomy attic) because it was near Fred's post office job. The ferry Walter

1931 **ANNUAL PICNIC** 1931

St. Paul's Lutheran Sunday School

South Eighth Street :: Allentown, Pa.

Central Park--Thursday, July 16, 1931

Featuring

WALTER CAMPBELL TETLEY

("Wee Sir Harry Lauder")

Free Milk

Ice Cream

Lolly Pops

Games

Contests

Specialties

The fourteen-year-old entertainer; well known on the Children's Hour from WJZ, will be with us in person; dressed in his Kilts, etc. You will have him with you all day and evening. This charming little fellow will sing for you both afternoon and evening. Paul Held will be his accompanist.

COME TO THE PICNIC — BRING YOUR FRIENDS — EVERYBODY WELCOME

We want as many as possible to be at the Park not later than 1.30 P.M. We will be in the lower Grove, near the Baseball Diamond.

(MASTER TETLEY IS PRESENTED THRU THE COURTESY OF THE NATIONAL BROADCASTING CO. ARTISTS SERVICE)

and his mother always took into New York was also only a short walk away. The boat crossing was at 125th Street and the fare was only a nickel.

At home, Walter kept two tie racks full of already-tied ties. One for everyday work (he was never without a bow or regular tie during working hours), and one group for Sundays. He kept a miniature figure of Captain Henry from his *Show Boat* series on top of the Sunday tie rack.

On April 5, 1932 Walter appeared as guest artist at the April Social of the Berean Bible Class at the First Baptist Church of Hackensack, New Jersey. His songs (about twenty-two numbers) and impersonations included "She's the Lass for Me," "Wiggle Waggle of the Kills," "Roamin' in the Gloaming," "My Bonnie Jean," "When I was Twenty-One," and "Flower of the Heather."

The Edgewater, New Jersey home.

Catching the ferry to work.

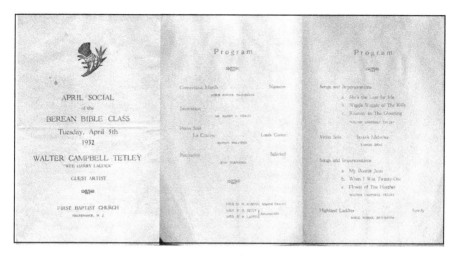

These were adult-type songs, to be sure, but they were the staples of his act, which he performed time and again. Such as at the Mother and Daughter Banquet at the Presbyterian Church in Morris Plains, New Jersey. The local paper called him the "bright spot" of the evening and wrote that he was "popular with everyone."

A Coaldale, Pennsylvania newspaper devoted an entire column to Walter's upcoming April 15th performance at the Coaldale High School Auditorium in aid of the Auspices Coaldale Relief Society. He appeared with two other *Children's Hour* stars. It's difficult to say how much of the highly complementary write-up was true, but it was great publicity to say that Walter studied algebra, French, English and Civics at

Walter and mother Tetley.

Walter Tetley To Show Here April 15th

Walter Campbell Tetley, the "wee Sir Harry Lauder" of radio and vaudeville, will appear here in person Friday, April 15th, at Coaldale High School Auditorium, in aid of Coaldale Relief Association. The concert is being arranged through the management of the NBC Artists Service and two additional stars of the Children's Hour will also be heard on the program.

WALTER CAMPBELL TETLEY

This tiny boy with sandy hair and clear blue-green eyes is of German and Scotch parentage. His mother was born in Glasgow, Scotland, while his father was brought to this country from Germany at an early age. Walter was born in New York City 12 years ago, but he is quite small for a boy of 12 years. He began singing at the age of five when his kindergarten teacher asked him to sing a Scotch song at a school party. He won, completely, the hearts of those who heard him and was greatly in demand for many affairs from that time on.

At the age of seven he was sent out with a group of children on a vaude...

N. J. C. CHILDREN'S HOUR CONCERT

Auspices Coaldale Relief Society

FRIDAY, EVENING APRIL 15, 1932

PROGRAMME.

COALDALE HIGH SCHOOL BAND.

(a) March: Spirit of Coaldale High .... John J. Burn
(b) Overture: Gypsy Festival .... Al Hayes

WALTER SCOTT

(a) Pampourin Chinois .... Kreisler
(b) Caprice Viennois .... Kreisler
(c) The Swan .... Saint-Saens
(d) Liebesfreud .... Kreisler

PEGGY ZINKE

First Appearance .... Dutch Impersonations

WALTER TETLEY

(a) She's The Lass for Me.
(b) Wiggle Waggle of the Kilt.

PEGGY ZINKE

Second Appearance .... French Impersonations

COALDALE HIGH SCHOOL BAND.

(a) First Movement Unfinished Symphony .... Schubert
(b) March: Good Fellowship .... F. O. Griffin

WALTER TETLEY

(a) When I Was Twenty-One.
(b) My Bonnie Jean.

PEGGY ZINKE

Third Appearance .... Irish Impersonations

WALTER SCOTT

(a) Hungarian Dance No. 1 .... Brahms
(b) Old Refrain .... Kreisler
(c) Vals Staccato .... Borrisson
(d) Dance of The Goblins .... Bazzini

PEGGY ZINKE

Fourth Appearance .... Readings

WALTER TETLEY

(a) Flower of the Heather
(b) The Message Boy

COALDALE HIGH SCHOOL BAND.

(a) Overture Mount Everest .... F. O. Griffin
(b) Stars and Stripes Forever .... Sousa
"Star Spangled Banner."

"a Professional Children's School in New York." He listed his hobbies as reading, especially the mystery thriller type (tops was Sherlock Holmes), and playing baseball. "Before I moved to New York," Walter explained, "I played baseball often. There were plenty of open spaces where we lived in New Jersey. I played pitcher and first base. Gee, I could throw curves, drops, slow balls and everything!"

He was usually catcher or first baseman in the game, when time allowed. He also enjoyed a good game of football with friends, though he had more time for a game of marbles in the studio between shows. He also collected match-covers—over 500 by August of 1937—and kept tropical fish, and dogs. Scrappy, his wire-haired terrier, came from a New Jersey kennel and cost $35. Sandy, a Scottish (of course!) terrier, cost $25 from a Brooklyn kennel. Both were thoroughbreds, though Walter's strong sense of charity would never have him buy a "designer" dog from a posh seller at a terrible price when there were poor dogs in need out there.

He also liked to carve and make items out of wood.

Walter and friends.

Almost all radio stars at the time were endorsing commercial items of some kind. Most of the time it was cigarettes. Young Walter was approached by the makers of Tootsie Rolls for a variety of magazine ads featuring the cameral product. "Radio stars, movies stars—men, women and children all over the country go for them in a big way. Have *you* tried a Tootsie today?" Walter supplied the already-taken photos which were typeset into energetic ads displaying the Tootsie Rolls. One later such advertisement appeared on the back cover of the July 24, 1937 issue of *Radio Guide*. That same magazine used another spread—with a different Tetley picture—also featuring Gus Arnheim and Jane Pickens in the August 14th issue, which hit newsstands on August 5th. It showed Walter in Scottish kit smiling and holding the NBC microphone. Along with a nice sized check, he was sent a box of Tootsie Rolls in appreciation.

Back in the studio, Walter was earning himself a reputation as a good supporting player to have around. One early radio review, probably in 1932, singled Walter out for his "astounding performance in a thrilling murder mystery drama to be sent over the air today and tomorrow by *The American Weekly*. The sketch is an adaptation of a true story in *The American Weekly*. It concerns a series of mysterious killings in which children are poisoned in their nurseries by a strange gas which is forced

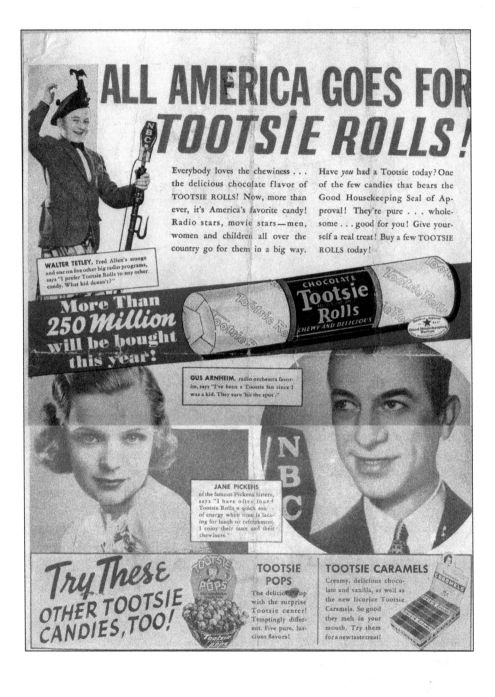

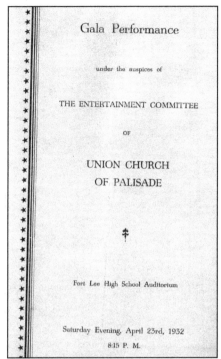

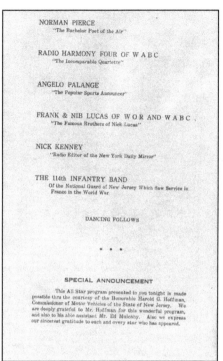

Gala Performance

under the auspices of

THE ENTERTAINMENT COMMITTEE

OF

UNION CHURCH

OF PALISADE

Fort Lee High School Auditorium

Saturday Evening, April 23rd, 1932

8:15 P. M.

NORMAN PIERCE
"The Bachelor Poet of the Air"

RADIO HARMONY FOUR OF W A B C
"The Incomparable Quartette"

ANGELO PALANGE
"The Popular Sports Announcer"

FRANK & NIB LUCAS OF W O R AND W A B C
"The Famous Brothers of Nick Lucas"

NICK KENNEY
"Radio Editor of the New York Daily Mirror"

THE 114th INFANTRY BAND
Of the National Guard of New Jersey Which Saw Service in France in the World War

DANCING FOLLOWS

* * *

SPECIAL ANNOUNCEMENT
This All Star program presented to you tonight is made possible thru the courtesy of the Honorable Harold G. Hoffman, Commissioner of Motor Vehicles of the State of New Jersey. We are deeply grateful to Mr. Hoffman for this wonderful program, and also to his able assistant Mr. Ed Mulcahy. Also we express our sincerest gratitude to each and every star who has appeared.

into the room."

And the personal appearances helped keep Walter Tetley's name on listeners' minds. On April 22, 1932 Walter sang his usual songs at the Memorial High School Band Concert, directed by William R. Reese at, of course, the Memorial High School auditorium in Kingston, Pennsylvania. As always, he was a smash.

The following night he appeared at a "Gala Performance under the auspices of the Entertainment Committee of Union Church of Palisade" at Fort Lee High School Auditorium, with Baby Rose Marie (of WEAF), Uncle Don (of WOR) and other radio acts. The Master of Ceremonies was the Honorable Harold G. Hoffman, Commissioner of Motor Vehicles of the State of New Jersey. The 8:15 p.m. Saturday night performance was followed by dancing.

For a whole quarter patrons could witness a "one-act play and chorus selections by members of the choir" with "assisting artists: Walter Tetley, well-known radio artist and star; Miss Grace Lang, 15-year-old Chinese pianist and winner in musical contests; Miss Vivian Donaldson, harpist" and others. Musical selections were played by the Edgewater Symphony

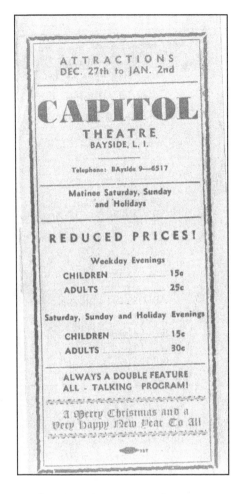

Orchestra. The evening began at 8:15 p.m. on Thursday, June 7th at the Eleanor Vangelder School.

Back on March 4, 1932 Walter had first appeared on *Friendship Town* as Laddie Stewart. Later that year, he got himself a "big sister" by the name of Margaret Stewart. She was brought in to perform Scottish, Irish and French songs. Harry Salter and his orchestra performed music for the series. The program was sponsored by the Chesebrough Manufacturing Company, which had a brief run on CBS, but quickly came back to NBC.

Walter shared the bill for the "N.B.C. Children's Hour Concert" with Peggy Zinke and Walter Scott. Tetley again performed his usual musical act: "She's the Lass For Me," "Wiggle Waggle of the Kill," "My Bonnie Jean," "When I Was Twenty-One," "Flower of the Heather," and also "The Message Boy." The review which followed the concert wrote that the

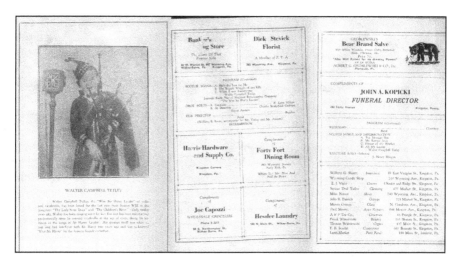

troupe "proved equal to any entertainers that ever visited the valley, and they met with wonderful success."

Walter Tetley ended 1932 by joining in a week-long run of "A Radio Review, a musical melody mélange" given at the Capitol Theatre in Bayside, New York on December 27-30. He joined "a cast of 20 leading radio artists in person from the principal eastern radio studios," including musical comedy and operatic star Joseph Ler Tora, a male quartette called The Four Grenadiers, the twin violists Mary and Virginia Dran, the vocal trio Three Little Maids, and others. Matinees were given daily beginning at 2 p.m. until 11 p.m.

From sharing so much limelight with his contemporaries it was obvious that fame was taking a long time to get to the little star's head. In fact, he never did become a "fat head."

IV

NOT JUST THE PERSONAL APPEARANCES, but the travel time involved took up a lot of Tetley's off-hours from radio. He appeared in a Woodland Hills, Pennsylvania variety show where he was once again singled out by the local reviewer. "On Sunday evening, a real treat is promised when Walter Tetley, the world's foremost juvenile Scotch entertainer will appear. This artist needs little introduction…"

By now he was a national name, though still a supporting player on radio. It was rumored that he had signed up for an extended vaudeville tour near the end of 1932, but his continuing radio work showed no signs of absenteeism.

Walter took part in an NBC-RKO extravaganza for the stage called *The R. K. Olians*, which featured mostly dancing (almost all fox trots with a few waltzes sprinkled in for variety's sake). Walter Campbell Tetley, under the direction of Frances Rockefeller King, was guest artist. Mr. Harry Meyer conducted the massive music show.

Around the same time, the second annual All-Star Radio Concert and Show was given on February 25, 1933 at Fort Lee High School in Fort Lee, New Jersey. It featured several NBC stars of the day, including Walter, baritone singer Phil Dewey, Genia Fonoriova ("famous Russian Mezzo-Soprano"), and "The Lady Next Door" herself (though she received no name credit; an odd bit of promotion that NBC would also do to Hal Peary). Dancers, more singers, comedians, the 115th Infantry Band, the Children's Radio League and other artists provided a gala evening.

March 8, 1933 was the date Tetley joined the cast of *Buck Rogers*, but it wasn't until October 3rd of that year that he became a regular cast member, as "Willie." Walter gave an abundance of auditions in this year,

NBC-RKO

Presents

"THE R. K. OLIANS"

Mr. Harry Meyer	Conductor
Walter Campbell Tetley	Guest Artist
Under direction of	Frances Rockefeller King

—— DANCE ORDER ——

1—Fox Trot—"Rise'n Shine" from "Take a Chance" ... Youmans	14—Fox Trot—"Hey! Young Feller" ... McHugh
2—Fox Trot—"If I Ever Get a Job Again" ... Baer	15—Waltz—"Play Fiddle Play" ... Altman
3—Fox Trot—"My Darling" ... Myers	16—Fox Trot—"Every Little Star" from "Music in the Air" ... Kern
4—Fox Trot—"Fit As a Fiddle" ... Goodhart	
5—Waltz—"Gems from 'Melody'" ... Romberg	INTERMISSION
6—Fox Trot—"You'll Get By" ... Coots	
7—Fox Trot—"At the Baby Parade" ... Schuster	17—Fox Trot—"Hits" from "Pardon My English" ... Gershwin
8—Fox Trot—"So I Married the Girl" ... Stept	18—Fox Trot—"Moon Song" ... Johnston
9—Fox Trot—"Louisiana Hayride" from "Flying Colors" ... Schwartz	19—Fox Trot—"Playing with Fire" ... Berlin
10—Waltz—"A Boy and a Girl Were Dancing" ... Revel	20—Waltz—"Rock-a-Bye Moon" ... Lang
11—Fox Trot—"Love Me Tonight" ... Rodgers	21—Fox Trot—"Here It is Monday" ... Cleary
12—Fox Trot—"Night and Day" from "Gay Divorce" ... Porter	22—Fox Trot—"Seven Little Steps to Heaven" ... Gensler
13—Fox Trot—"Sittin' by the Fire With You" ... Wendling	23—Fox Trot—"Willow Weep For Me" ... Ahlert
	24—Waltz—"I Wake Up Smiling" ... Hupfeld
	25—Fox Trot—"Just So You'll Remember" ... Meyer

especially in June. The day after one of these the little actor joined the cast of *Winnie-the-Pooh* as the invigorated, bouncy stuffed animal "Tigger." This children's serial was heard over the NBC-WEAF network each Wednesday and Friday at 5:30 p.m. The A.A. Milne stories were adapted by Elizabeth Todd of the NBC continuity department.

At Washington's First Annual Radio and Electric Show that same year Walter was joined by Martha Attwood of the Metropolitan Opera Company, Dr. John Bellamy Taylor (demonstrating his famous "House of Magic," which showed sound waves being converted into light), and master of ceremonies John S. Young, NBC announcer. William S. Abernathy, local WRC announcer, introduced the acts which were also broadcast over WRC. Over 3,500 people attended the first night's show (which Walter did not attend), and over 4,000 the next night. 17-year-old Walter's age was listed as 11 and 12 in several local papers publicizing the event.

Another paper during the same time listed his age as thirteen. It also claimed that "when he is not broadcasting Walter Tetley likes best to climb mountains. But he doesn't have much spare time" due to his three hit series now running simultaneously: *Raising Junior* (over WJZ), *The Children's Hour* (Sunday mornings from 9 to 10, where he sang Scottish songs) and the stalwart *The Lady Next Door*.

Meantime *Buck Rogers* was appealing to critics and audiences alike. One March 1933 review wrote: "In purchasing this long-run serial Cream of Wheat is relinquishing Alexander Woollcott and making a snappy bid for the kids who go on a hot-cereal diet in winter. *Buck Rogers* has all the trimmings for a two-fisted knockdown, drag out job. Story, scripted by E.R. Johnstone, fabricates a lot of synthetic adventure which takes place in inter-stellar space 500 years in the future. Lines and pace serve only one purpose—to get as racy as possible—and to that extent admirably suit their ends. Odd voices and weird sound effects (most of the latter poorly done) creep in. Aside from the adventure lure, there is a thick condiment of pseudo-scientific terms." The best component of the series, the reviewer stated, was the cast which "ably sells its stuff the way the layout calls for. Will probably move a good bit of cereal off grocers' shelves."

The commercials themselves were fun. For the price of a box top off a Cream of Wheat box little listeners could join a club to become a "solar scout" and be "a personal friend of Buck Rogers." Members received a gold badge and handbook. Cream of Wheat was touted as "what's needed to succeed."

On July 19, 1933 it was announced to the press that Walter would be playing Stephen Foster (age 6-9) on John Tasker Howard's series on the noted American folksong writer. Broadcast Wednesday evenings on NBC-WEAF at 8:30 p.m. E.S.T., it contained many of Foster's classic melodies as played and sung by an orchestra and quartet directed by NBC music executive Thomas Belviso. Laddie Seaman portrayed young Foster as a 14-to-19-year-old, but at the time the series had not yet progressed far enough to need to cast the adult Foster role. According to the record Walter's parents kept, Tetley had portrayed the first part of this two-part Foster show on July 12, 1933. Walter would also be heard on the air as Babe Ruth, Jack Dempsey, the Barrymores and Richard Barthelmess in their boyhood days.

On Maxwell House's *Show Boat* Walter played the blind waif, newsboy Eddie, who wandered onto the Showboat and was "adopted" by Lanny Ross and the Show Boat troupe. He began the role on August 24, 1933. Heard over the NBC-WEAF network Thursday nights at 9 p.m., Walter was signed to a 52-week contract for this series. At the same time he signed a 26-week contract to support Helen Hayes in her new radio series which was to commence on October 8th.

Being a typical young boy, in rare free moments away from the microphone, Walter was apt to get into some innocent mischief. If given an opportunity, he would ride the Radio City studios' pianos as porters moved them from studio to studio between programs. He also enjoyed

Tetley playing for corn's sake.

seeking out unusual or hidden places throughout the studios: in the air-conditioning duct, the battery room, the master control board, or in the basement watching engineers work their magic.

But then he found *real* magic in the person of Ray Kelly, chief of the sound effects department. He would often talk to Kelly about the various contraptions he used to produce all the sounds, and Walter relished in being shown examples. Whenever he would walk in for a session of learning, the first thing Walter would do was to blow the huge whistle that opened and closed every *Show Boat* program.

Walter found himself on a series called *Main Street* on September 24, 1933. He would appear on the serial-type show now and then as son Wilbur of the Higgins family. The cast included Don Carney (later famous for his Uncle Don show) as Luke Higgins, Edith Spencer as his wife Sary, Wally Maher as Ezra, Alan Bunce as Jack, Doro Merande as Ivalutty, Robert Strauss as Horace, and Florence Halop as Fanny.

When *The Wizard of Oz* needed a lad to play Tip, on November of 1933, 100 amateurs were tried out. None of them worked. In the end, they chose a seasoned workhorse: Walter Tetley. Using his best "12-year-old voice," he began appearing on the series as on November 15, 1933.

During the latter half of 1933 when NBC moved to Radio City, Walter appeared as one of the entertainers to launch the new place of business. He was later thanked by John F. Royal of NBC for his "enthusiastic cooperation on the occasion. Our opening week was a great success in no small measure due to your participation." He was also applauded by managing director George Engles: "The spirit which caused you to so unselfishly give of your time, is in my opinion, in keeping with this new era of broadcasting which comes into being with our move to Radio City."

NBC was so proud of their junior star that sometimes they loaned him out to rival networks, as was the case in June of 1934 when he "was heard Monday night with the big show over the Columbia broadcasting station with Mady Christian." Also included in the 9:30 p.m. performance were Helen Menken (co-star of *Mary of Scotland*), the "exotic blues singer" Gertrude Niesen, and Erno Rapee and His Orchestra.

1933 came to an end with several other new series for little Tetley. He briefly joined Jane and Goodman Ace in their quarter-hour comedy series, *Easy Aces*; and began *Bobby Benson's Adventures*, also on CBS, on Christmas Eve. Walter appeared as Jock and often appeared in kilt to promote the series. His Scottish photograph was even given away as a radio premium for the series. Though his main appearances were in January of 1934 he would sporadically appear on the series when another youth was needed.

Town Hall with Fred Allen
The Sun
Uncle Abe & David
Unemployed
Walter Winchell
Welch with Irene Rich
White Owl with Burns & Allen
Wizard of Oz
Woodbury with Paul Whiteman
Radio Album

The Great Jasper
True Story
Under Wood
Vick Open House
Wayside Cottage
Wheatenaville
Winnie the Pooh
Womens Radio Review
Star Dust

Stars I Work With

Maud Adams
John Battle
Ethel John & Lional Barrymore
Louisa M Alcott
Eddie Cantor
Jack Dempsey
Amelia Earhart
Block & Sully
Gertrude Niasen
George Price
Ripley
Wheeler & Woolsey
B.A.Rolfe
Charles Winninger
Babe Ruth
Joe Penner
Mary Livingston
Marx Brothers
Sizzlers
Fred Rich
Roxy
Guy Lambardo
Raymond Knight
Portland Hooper

Fred Allen
Burns & Allen
Jack Benny
Mady Chistians
Clarence Darrow
Spence Dean
Mitzie Green
Carlson Robinson
Johnny Hart
George Jessel
Fred Waring
Paul Whiteman
Leslie Howard
Grace Moore
Irene Rich
Jerry Mann
Walter Winchell
Warden Laws
Borah Minnevitch
Lanny Ross
George Givot
McIntrye
Ace Goodman

The credit list mounts…

V

1934 WAS A SIGNIFICANT YEAR in Walter Tetley's life. On January 4th he had his first appearance with Fred Allen, on the half-hour *Sal Hepatica Revue*. Ultimately Allen was the man who would take Walter to the other coast where he would remain for the rest of his life.

As one of Allen's Alley Players, Walter was signed on in the part of a sassy brat named Waldo. It significantly showed the world that this kid could play comedy. It gave him the perfect venue to showcase his versatility with dialects and voices and served as a perfect foil to Allen's wry, caustic delivery. Though he was only with the series until the end of 1937, he had picked up a lot of "wise-cracking" skill that would serve him well in future high-profile series.

It was also in 1934 that Tetley toured the music halls of Britain with his "Wee Sir Harry" act for seven weeks in the summer, from July 1 to August 17. He and his mother sailed aboard the *Caledonia*, paying for their passages by Walter performing during both voyages. Theatres in London, Newcastle, Glasgow, Edinburgh and others were excited about his act which was decidedly closer to home than the United States. In fact, one of the reasons he couldn't do a tour of this size in the United States was due to restrictions imposed by the Gerry Society, also known as the New York Society for the Prevention of Cruelty to Children, founded in 1875 by Henry Bergh. But of course a United Kingdom tour delighted the Scots, and Mrs. Tetley, who had very much wanted to see the old homeland.

Because of his tireless work in a kilt, on July 26, 1934 Walter was made a member of the Daily Record Scottish Chum Club, registered as Chum No. 392455. Sir Harry Lauder was already a member. Walter's Chum Club certificate was signed by "Uncle Jack" and boasted the rules of the club:

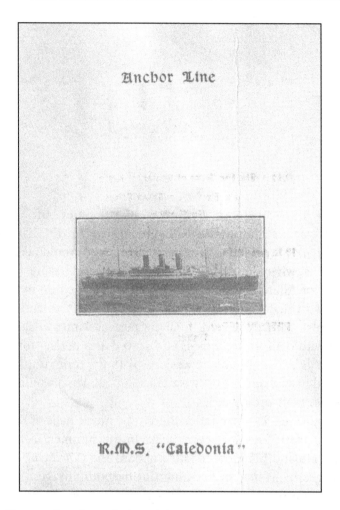

Anchor Line

R.M.S. "Caledonia"

1. A Chum is bright and cheerful.
2. A Chum is thoughtful of others.
3. A Chum tries to help those less fortunate or in trouble.
4. A Chum does his or her best to assist the Chum Club schemes.
5. A Chum is always kind to animals, and protects them from ill-treatment.
6. A Chum resolves to do his or her best for Scotland.

"The Rules of the Chum Club are simple and few. And easy to keep if you're honest and true." Anyone who followed Walter's rigorous charity performances knew that Walter fit right in on those counts.

On the return trip of August 15th Walter joined other entertainers (Rev. Father Bell, Miss M. Prunty and Mr. H. Hammond) for a program

of fun, variety and dancing aboard the *H.M.S. Caledonia*. Messrs. Black and Hughan were emcees for the gay cruise which also sported a buffet supper of sandwiches, hot dogs, and ice cream and wafers.

Naturally, Walter's first radio credit upon returning to work on August 18th was *Lady Next Door*. Many more episodes of *Children's Hour, Fred Allen, Buck Rogers, Eno Crime Club*, auditions and other shows followed.

Apart from a successful tour, Walter also came back with gold in hand, in the form of several new songs written for him by Harry Lauder's own ballad writer, J. Hall Nicol.

One such song that Walter had bought outright, "Flora," went thusly:

1. A nice wee lass is Flora
The Lass I'm coortin' noo,
A soorock frae the Hielans'
She's my Bonnie Cushie Doo.
Tae ramble through the heather
Wi' this lass I never tire.
I'll need tae jine the Fire Brigade,
She set my heart on fire.

Chorus:
My wee Scots Darlin,
Is Flora McIntyre,
A lump o' Hielan honey,
She's the lassie I admire,
Reared among the heather hills,
Her cheeks are like the rose,
Ye could hang yer Tam o'Shanter
On her wee pug nose.

2. I'll no forget the summer day,
I met this pretty maid,
We strolled amang the heather,
An' I rowed her in my plaid,
Says she tae me behave yersel,
Ye'll mak me rin awa,
Ye'd better see a barber,
Fer yer whiskers' like a saw.

3. Flora's goin' tae merry me,
She's fixed the day in Spring,
I've saved up one and sixpence,
For tae buy the wedding ring,
Tae drive us tae the minister,
I'll get a Coach an' pair,
A coal cart or a lorry,
For she's worth it a' and mair.

He also returned sporting a golf bag which was such a personal prize that he refused to let others carry it. He learned the game of golf on the wonderful rolling hills of Scotland during off days. Walter still found outdoor pursuits more to his liking, especially after being cooped up in studios and theatres. Growing a little older, a love of horseback riding, fishing and golf began to take the place of baseball and football in his heart.

In October of 1934 Walter began appearing more regularly on *American School of the Air*, as part of the "Hamilton Family" segment, playing one of the three sons who learned their geography lessons as they visited various locales.

```
                    Flera.
                 ------------

1  A nice wee lags is Flera
       The Lass I'm coortin'nee,
   A seereek grae the Hielams'
       She's my Bennie Cushie Dee.
   Tae ramble though the heather
       Wi' this lass I never tire.
   I,ll need tae jine the Fire Brigade,
       She set my heart on fire

                 Cherus :-
                 -----------

       My wee Scots Darlin,
       Is Flera McIntyre,
       A lump e' Hielam heney,
       She's the lassie I admire,
       Reared among the heather hills,
       Her cheeks are like the rose,
       Ye could hang yer Tam e'Shanter
       On har wee pug nose

2  I'll ne forget the summer day,
       I met this pretty maid,
   We strelled amang the heather,
       An' I rowed her in my plaid,
   Says she tae me behave yersel,
       Ye'll mak me rin awa,
   Ye'd better see a barber,
       Fer yer whiskers' like a saw.

3. Flera's goin' tae merry me,
       She's fixed the day in Spring,
   I've saved up ene and sixpence,
       Fer tae buy the wedding ring,
   Tae drive us tae the minister,
       I'll get a Ceach an' pair,
   A ceal cart er a lerry,
       Fer she' werth it a' and mair.

                    Written, Cempesed
                    By J. Hall Nisel,
                       Fer
                    Walter Campbell Tetley
                    Cepyright.
```

The man/kid was expanding his resume of credits with a rapidity that never really tapered off until he hit his main series, *The Great Gildersleeve*. He was one popular boy. During the mid-1930's one reviewer wrote of him: "At one rehearsal of an Eddie Cantor program, I recall seeing Tetley, not only winning plaudits from Cantor for the way he was handling his lines, but even walking off with another kid's part after the latter fluffed repeatedly." His dedication to perfection—and the old adage, "do a professional job, and you'll get asked back"—was the key to his success. It was even reported that Walter once cracked his kneecap just before a broadcast, but he still went on without faltering.

He reportedly appeared on Edgar Bergen's program, though that credit was not listed by his father. Also on *The Rudy Vallee Show* (WEAF, 8-9 p.m.) he supported Boris Karloff in a drama entitled "There's Always Joe Winters."

One newspaper stated in the mid or late 1930s that Walter was earning nearly $1,000 a month from his numerous broadcasts. Mainly due to the zealous nature of Walter's manager-mother who had hiked Walter's acting fees up 600%—because she could get it.

VI

AFTER WALTER HAD RETURNED from his UK tour NBC announced in the fall of 1934 that their favorite little supporting player would finally have his chance at a lead role. *Thrills of Tomorrow*, a 15-minute dramatic series for boys, was launched on Friday October 19th over the NBC-WEAF network at 6 p.m. E.S.T. The A.C. Gilbert Company sponsored the show which visualized the part "inventions of today may play in the everyday life of tomorrow." Walter played Spike Butler, "eager and curious in dramas of seadromes, combination airplanes and dirigibles, recovery of gold from the ocean's floor and other exciting possibilities of the future. No fantastic or improbable feats will be presented in the series, and each broadcast will deal with a scientific venture regarded as feasible by recognized engineers."

Written by Raymond Scudder, the first episode dealt with "the possibilities of seadromes spaced at 500-mile intervals across the ocean."

COMIC WALTER TETLEY

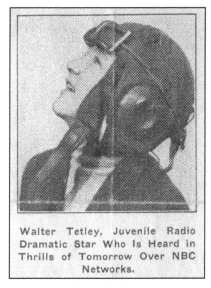

Walter Tetley, Juvenile Radio Dramatic Star Who Is Heard in Thrills of Tomorrow Over NBC Networks.

Walter Tetley in the NBC series, *Thrills of Tomorrow*.

MEN'S CLUB
ASTORIA PRESBYTERIAN CHURCH
33rd Street, between Broadway and Jamaica Ave

NINE REELS MOTION PICTURE VIEWS

"SCOTLAND"

ENTERTAINMENT

Wee Walter Tetley
Radio Star

Dan Hood
Comedian

and others
Direction: BRUCE CRANSTON

THURSDAY MARCH 14, 1935
8 P. M. SHARP

Admission - 25c

BILTMORE THEATRE
ELBERT SEVERANCE, Manager

FIRE NOTICE: The exit, indicated by a red light and sign, nearest to the seat you occupy, is the shortest route to the street.
In the event of fire or other emergency please do not run—WALK TO THAT EXIT.
JOHN J. McELLIGOTT, Fire Chief and Commissioner

SUNDAY EVENING, MAY 5, 1935

THE THEATRICAL CHILDREN'S ASSOCIATION,
UNDER THE AUSPICES OF
THE PROFESSIONAL CHILDREN'S SCHOOL, 1860 BROADWAY
PRESENT A

MONSTER ALL STAR BENEFIT
(Authorized by Theatre Authority, Inc.)

FOR THE NEEDY CHILDREN OF THE PROFESSIONAL CHILDREN'S SCHOOL

THE FOLLOWING ARTISTS HAVE PROMISED TO APPEAR:

Victor Moore	Vaughn De Leath
Ray Perkins	Milton Berle
Joe Penner and Duck	Frankie Thomas
Nick Kenny	Walter Tetley
Saxon Sisters	Mary Small
The Sizzlers	Jolly Bill & Jane
Cameron Andrews	Ted Claire
Jack Pearl	Roxy
Bob Hope	Martha Raye
Pete the Dog	Keep Moving
Maurine & Norva	Billy Halop (Billy Benson)

Al Bernie
And Many, Many Others

Ted Claire as permanent Master of Ceremonies
Music supplied by George Vittner and his Orchestra

Spike Butler was joined in his adventuring by Pete Farley, played by Ned Weaver.

As 1935 came around, Walter's personal appearances were still going strong. At the Astoria Presbyterian Church on 33rd Street in New York City the Men's Club presented a "Scotland" night which of course had to include wee Walter Tetley, joined by comedian Dan Hood. Bruce Cranston directed the March 13, 1935 show which also included a 9-reel motion picture "view of Scotland." The performance began at 8 p.m. SHARP. Admission was a quarter.

On a Sunday evening on May 5, 1935 Walter took part in one of the biggest celebrity charity shows of his career. The Monster All-Star Benefit, authorized by Theatre Authority, Inc., was presented by the Theatrical Children's Association, "under the auspices of the Professional Children's School" at 1860 Broadway in New York City, "for the needy children of the

CONCERT

FOR THE BENEFIT OF THE

FIRST PRESBYTERIAN CHURCH

Edgewater, New Jersey

AT THE ELEANOR VAN GELDER SCHOOL

MAY 23, 1935 at 8 P. M.

PROGRAM

My Lovely Celia .... Higgins
Rosalie .... DeKoven
Thank God for a Garden .... Del Riego
ERNEST LATOWSKY, Tenor
Florence Hubbart at the Piano

By the Beautiful Blue Danube .... Strauss—Schulz—Evler
MIRIAM SHIELDS, Pianist

Spring's Awakening .... Sanderson
BERTHA TANNER RICHARDS, Soprano
Ellmer Zoller at the Piano

Tanzerin von Sevilla .... Grunow
Ave Maria .... Schubert
Dance of the Goblins .... Bazzini
YOICHI HIRAOKA, Xylophonist
Miriam Shields at the Piano

She's the Lass for Me .... Lauder
Wiggle Waggle o' the Kilt .... Lauder
WALTER TETLEY, Juvenile Harry Lauder

To Sevilla .... Dessauer
Standchen .... Schubert
ERNEST LATOWSKY

Vo Mine Berge Muss i Scheide .... Swiss Folk-song
S'trotzig Dirndel .... Heinze
BERTHA TANNER RICHARDS, American Swiss Soprano

Bag-pipe Solo
The Trousers that ma Faither Used to Wear .... Mills
Whistle in the Thistle .... Burke
WALTER TETLEY

Andanti from "Surprise" Symphony .... Haydn
La Serenata .... Tosti
Second Hungarian Rhapsody .... Liszt
YOICHI HIRAOKA

Professional Children's School." Ted Claire was the Master of Ceremonies leading a stellar cast including Victor Moore, Joe Penner and Duck, Jack Pearl, Bob Hope, Milton Berle, Billy Halop, Martha Raye and many others. Music was supplied by George Vistner and his orchestra.

Later that month the First Presbyterian Church of Edgewater, New Jersey invited their Walter for a benefit concert given at the Eleanor Van Gelder School on May 23, 1935 at 8 p.m. It was a musical evening, with songs from xylophonist Yoichi Hiraoka, tenor Ernest Latowsky, and soprano Bertha Tanner Richards. Walter sang some of his regulars, plus a few new songs brought back from the UK. After a bagpipe solo he entertained the audience with "The Trousers That Me Father Used to Wear," "Whistle in the Thistle" and others.

Also that month a pleasant article appeared in *Radioland*, giving evidence to Walter's breadth and stamina: "Perhaps the most promising comedian of the future is a fourteen-year-old lad—Walter Tetley of *Buck Rogers* and *Bar X Days* fame, who has been a featured radio player for eight years. Walter is amazingly mature and workmanlike, switching from character to character with the ease and deftness of a Ted Bergman. Watching him in a rehearsal of the Fred Allen show, of which cast he is a regular member, it was surprising to see him portray five different characters in three different dialects in the space of a half hour.

"From the Allen rehearsal he rushed to an adjoining studio where Miss Tucker was putting her kids through their paces for the Sunday morning *Children's Hour*. She requested Walter to sing one of the songs he had brought back from Europe after an extensive tour through the British Isles, preferably one with patter in some dialect to serve as a setting for the number. Walter replied casually, 'I haven't one with patter, but I can write some in.' And write some in he did right there in the control room. Many a highly-paid comedian tearing his hair for new ideas and gags would have been proud to admit ownership to the Cockney monologue this fourteen-year-old prodigy dashed off so glibly."

On July 7, 1935 Walter was heard as guest artist on *Star Dust* over WAAT. He appeared in the Hotel Plaza ballroom dressed in kilt, carrying his bagpipes. He also performed an original comedy song, accompanied by Jay Stanley on the piano, in which he had to use eight different dialects, including his usual English, Cockney, French, Italian, German and Irish. And then he did a first for *Star Dust*: he played those bagpipes. After the performance he was besieged by fans and spent the next half hour signing autographs.

In early July he also began regular appearances on *The Simpson Boys*, "at Sprucehead Bay, in which he is heard as that incorrigible little rascal, Otie Bean." It was a weekly half-hour series on NBC starring Parker Fennelly and Arthur Allen. Early titles for the show were *Snow Village Sketches, The Stebbins Boys* and *Uncle Abe & David*.

The summer of this year saw busy Tetley racing from radio show to vaudeville house, playing all the theatres within commuting distance to New York so he would never have to miss a radio broadcast. His new stage act gave Walter the opportunity to sing in Scottish, Jewish and cockney dialects. He also began assisting his patter writer Arthur Behim in writing the material.

It was around the fall of '35 when Walter had to drop out of the seventh grade due to the grueling radio work that left him no time for personal appearances at his *own* high school. But a tutor had been hired to continue his education and get him ready for college. He excelled in French, causing his tutor to report that his ear for accents was so keen, he could have been a French instructor. The fact that Tetley was 20 years old in 1935 either meant the article that reported this fact was fed the wrong birth date (the most probable reason), or Mrs. Tetley kept Walter's true age a secret even from his own school.

Walter was scheduled to appear at a Newark theatre in the Fall, but his weeks were already full: *Buck Rogers* on Mondays, Tuesdays and Wednesdays at 6 p.m., and *Bobby Benson* on Mondays, Wednesdays and Fridays at 6:15 p.m. Somehow he managed to fill in the odd gaps with appearances on the shows of Joe Penner, Burns and Allen, Jack Benny and George Givot. *Buck Rogers* was his favorite program at the time, one of the reasons being that series author Jack Johnstone also did the sound effects on the show. Walter got a kick out of the electric shaver that made the sound for the "noise from another world."

One thing that all newspaper reports agreed on at the time was that 15 (really 20) year old Walter had boundless energy. "Engaging, friendly and wholesome" were words found more often than not in the press, and all were deeply pleased at Walter's unaffected nature. For all his success, he remained unspoiled and the epitome of that little kid (minus the accents) he continued to play.

An article in the *Sullivan County Republican* related one reporter's sit in with Walter on an October 1935 episode of *Bobby Benson's Adventures*. He was amazed at the wealth these kids made and the busy lives they led at such a young age. "I wonder if their thousands of little listeners can believe that when Bobby (Billy Halop) says leisurely 'HO Oats for the kid who knows his oats' he has his hat and coat on and is half out the door in his haste to rush off, I assumed, to another child program elsewhere." Bobby, a good friend of Walter's at that time, had been on the air since he was 4 years old.

The reporter also spent time with Walter's mother who was only too eager to tell the press of her son's many radio credits. "I don't suppose she meant his salary to be published but I must admit I was floored when she told me what he earns in a week."

It was still profitable to be a kid. On December 1st he proved that yet another way by regularly appearing on *Funnies*, a weekly Sunday morning show on which comic strips were read over the air.

VII

IN A 1936 INTERVIEW, WALTER STATED, "I started in show business when I was five years old doing a single act in vaudeville. I was seven when my mother was working on a case as a registered nurse and the mother of the little girl she was taking care of knew that I was working. She suggested that I do some radio work and got me an audition with NBC. The next thing I knew I was singing Scottish songs on *The Children's Hour* over WJZ New York every Sunday morning."

It was due to Mrs. Tetley that Walter was now making well beyond the $100 a week he had been getting for his constant radio work. He owed his entire career to his mother who saw to it that his talent was always encouraged and showcased. Obviously Walter liked the show biz arena and publicly never had an unkind word to say against his determined mother, though she could ruffle feathers. Arthur Anderson wrote in his book *Let's Pretend*: "One of the best-organized and most aggressive stage mothers was Walter Tetley's. For years, until Walter finally moved to the West Coast, any director getting off the elevator on NBC's third floor knew that he would probably have to run a one-woman gauntlet with flaming red frizzy hair and steel-rimmed glasses consisting of Mrs. Tetley, who would accost him with, 'Don't you have anything for Walter today?'"

Even those who ordinarily didn't like working with kids found it hard to resist Walter's professionalism. Jack Johnstone, author of Walter's series *Buck Rogers* and later, *The Treasure Adventures of Jack Masters*, confessed his hatred of working with children, but singled out Walter as one of a kind.

Walter was also expertly complimented upon his performance in *The New Penny*, starring Helen Hayes. In 1936 Helen's father wrote the star of *The New Penny* (Helen), suggesting that the show just wasn't worth listening to without Walter in it. That and a volume of other fan mail convinced the powers that be to write Walter back into the script quickly, with Walter as "Mickey" in a new storyline.

The New Penny was broadcast at 9:30 Tuesday nights on the Blue Network out of studio 3-E. Rehearsals were usually done on the preceding Monday between 3 and 4 p.m. Its sponsor was Sanka. Edith Meiser wrote the scripts, usually "knitting away on a sweater. But, every once in a while, without lifting her head, she adds some pertinent comment which is quickly noted by the artist referred to." Joe Stauffer, a graduate of West Point, directed, and the announcer was Bill Adams. Tom McKnight, Mesier's manager, also functioned as production manager for the program, while the engineer was John Kulick. Around the end of December 1935 star Helen Hayes had refused an offer of $100,000 to do a film, preferring to stay with her series. "I place my home before any career," she said at the time. "Radio affords me the opportunity to remain near my family and yet be in the center of all theatrical activities—New York."

Part of the reason for the success of many child actors was due to the parental and ethical guidance he or she received. Mrs. Tetley was the family driving power, but also businesswoman and schmoozer, even long after little Walter had been established. She would still accompany him to every broadcast and immediately upon entering the studio, she would switch from mother to business manager. Yet she never went into an audition or rehearsal with the young actor.

"In my generation," she told reporters, "children were raised to be seen and not heard. But that wouldn't be very good radio training for a child. So I have brought Walter up on the theory that parents should not be seen – or heard. I try never to put myself forward. Some of the stars who are very fond of Walter-Leslie Howard and Helen Hayes for instance—wouldn't even recognize me if they saw me."

She taught him how not to have an ego as well, to consider the audience's wishes before his own. Walter also never minded signing autographs after a performance. Though he would have much preferred to be off playing ping-pong with the studio page boys.

When something important cropped up, Walter would be snatched from parties or holidays for an unscheduled broadcast or rehearsal. But the young man never complained. He loved the work.

In one of the few articles on Walter in a radio magazine, the little actor listed his ten do's and don'ts for being a success in radio:

1. Don't be late, for broadcasts or rehearsals.
2. Don't disappear after you get there. The director may have important notes. Don't get in his way either.
3. Know your part. Don't lose your script or your place.
4. Concentrate on the show – not sweets, nor the girls.
5. Do what you were hired for: reading lines, not playing the trombone.
6. Do what you're told, how you're told to do it. The director directs, the actor acts.
7. Dogs, roller skates and mothers must be kept out in the hall.
8. Don't ad lib unless you've been instructed to. Timing is everything.
9. Show your fans love, and respect. They control your present and future.
10. Don't act your age, but don't forget it! Don't call your elders by their first names, unless told otherwise.

He learned those rules through experience, and practiced them diligently. But when the show was over, he was a boy again. One press release suggested that he loved helping with hats and coats in the studio check room: his favorite past-time between broadcasts.

But away from the studio, when he wasn't going to a ball game (sometimes getting pointers from Babe Ruth beforehand), he had seven pet turtles, horses and a 33-foot speedboat cabin cruiser to keep him busy. But the boat's christening had had to be postponed when it "interfered" with the initial appearance in New York of another great ship—the Queen Mary. "Uncle Jim" Harkins from *Town Hall Tonight* and Irene Rich were invited over for the christening. Irene did the honors, but not with a bottle of champagne—with grape juice. NBC executives felt that the christening and launching should be broadcast, and so it was.

Soon Walter was inviting friends over to cruise the New Jersey waterways. His friend and fellow actor Frank McIntyre, Captain Henry of *Show Boat*, was one of the first invited for a spin in the new craft. But the trip did not last long due to Captain Henry's bout with acute seasickness.

How Walter could be old enough to have a license for the craft and still be touted as a "kid" was unimportant and ignored.

He could afford the vessel, though. The "boy" was now bringing in $300 a week.

Walter and unknown friend taking the boat for a spin.

Around 1935/36 Walter was elected vice-president of an adult dramatic club in Edgewater, New Jersey, where he still lived. At his Roosevelt School, where he had won a five-dollar gold piece for being best speller, a song he wrote had been selected as Class Song.

In fact, the first five dollars Tetley ever received from a radio performance he gave to a fund to build President Roosevelt a swimming pool. He had real affection for Roosevelt, as Walter had had infantile paralysis when he was a baby. Sympathy for those in ill health was a trait that never left Walter. For years, ever since he was five years old, he performed in an annual show at the Crippled Children's Hospital in New York City. Nothing would make him break that date.

VIII

As of 1935 Walter was still getting raves for his wee Lauder act. The *Albany Evening News* thought "his impersonation of a Scotch youngster on a recent Allen broadcast was magnificent. The burr was not overdone, as is generally the case. Indeed, all of this lad's efforts, so far as I'm concerned, are quite satisfactory. I think he ranks right up there with the best of the best..."

But by now he was getting a little tired of his Scots act. He didn't want to be completely typecast as a dialect comedian. As an article at the time stated, "when he stepped into it six years ago, he was so well received on radio and stage that he didn't know it would grow irksome by the time he put on long pants and began to have aspirations to a stage career for life." If anything he was grateful for the plethora of work that was coming his way. To a kid who had to work through his childhood, who was never really allowed to grow up, all of the audio work allowed him a constant change of pace and character. He never grew bored.

On the contrary, there were some real perks to being NBC's number one "boy." He loved to go horseback riding. And what kind of kid would he be without a stab at offstage practical jokes? Tetley would buy tricks like an artificial fly he liked to wear on his coat lapel to lure the 'shoos' of his friends; not to mention running around with water pistols.

And as the dark days of the Depression crept on, his NBC salary crept up. $350 a week was rather good, regardless of the hours spent at his craft. And every Saturday night Mrs. Tetley would give her son $3.50 spending money, banking the rest and taking care of expenses. "He's remarkably talented," she admitted, "but that's no reason for letting too much money spoil him." There were a few times, though, when Walter managed "to fool mother. I save up for a couple of weeks and then I go on a real spree."

Though she served as his manager, she did it under the supervision of the National Broadcasting Company who managed his radio activities.

Between Jessie and NBC, Walter was never without a new audition or public appearance to attend, formerly sanctioned by the radio company who always required credit in his billing.

Jessie would accompany her son to every broadcast he gave at Radio City. She would also see him on and off stage during his vaudeville and other appearances, such as his recent Plymouth Theater performances. Between shows he would have French, English, civics and algebra lessons to study with his tutor who usually accompanied him. But when she couldn't get away, Walter would do them by correspondence.

"Sure, it's hard work," Walter admitted. "But I don't care, so long as I can be an actor. On the road, I don't care if I don't have regular meals, if the dressing rooms are cold or stuffy, or if I don't make a lot of money. But I've got to be an actor."

His performance at the Plymouth Theatre lasted three days. The headline act was the Eva Phillips Review, which contained deluxe ballroom dancing and "sensational acrobatic work." The seven-act vaudeville show also included the Robert DePerron Duo, a balancing act; Smith, Rogers and Eddy, comics and dancers; Walter C. Tetley, "radio's boy wonder comedian"; Saul Brilliant, "late star of nothing"; and Murray "Hats" Parker. It was followed by the film *Front Page Woman* starring Bette Davis and George Brent.

1936 was indeed a good year. Walter had been named Outstanding Child Actor in Radio for the previous year, and more series were lined up.

After several auditions for Hi Brown, on January 30, 1936 Tetley began appearing on *News of Youth*, a quarter-hour show broadcast on Monday, Wednesday and Friday from WABC's Studio #4 in New York City. The NBC series aired from 6:15 to 6:30 p.m. and was sponsored by the Ward Baking Company. The program held a solid cast of children and was produced by Hi Brown and Raymond Knight, the latter of which had produced *The Cuckoo Hour*.

Other 1936 series that began to crop up more frequently included *Death Valley Days*, a half-hour weekly drama about the old west; the hot crime drama, *Gang Busters*; *Renfrew of the Mounted*, or *Tales of the Canadian Mounted Police*, a half-hour series on CBS; *March of Time*, a weekly documentary-type show; *Old Dr. Jim*, a quarter-hour daily soap opera; and *The Treasure Adventures of Jack Masters*. He also showed up on episodes of *The Kate Smith Show*, *We the People*, *Home, Sweet, Home*, and at times (so it was reported) he substituted for Johnny, the calling pageboy for Phillip Morris cigarette commercials.

As of June 1936 Walter's "permanent address" was given as 5 Beverly Place, Edgewater, New Jersey. A promotional page taken out in *Billboard* showed his versatility by listing his various shows. The kid had a full week: *Paul Whiteman*, 9:30 p.m. Sundays; *Buck Rogers*, 6 p.m. Mondays, Wednesdays and Fridays; *Bobby Benson*, 6:15 p.m. Mondays, Wednesdays and Fridays; *Fred Allen* 9 p.m. Wednesdays; *Show Boat* 9 p.m. Thursdays. It was reported this time that he was making $700 a week and got a dollar allowance.

On January 14, 1937 Walter portrayed young Herbert and Harry Schryver in the Fanny Foote story for sponsor Floyd Gibbons' *Colgate True Adventure*.

He kept up his usual series, plus had appearances on *Captain Diamond* (stories of a lighthouse keeper for NBC), Joe Cook's show, *Circus Night in Silvertown*, and lots of *Ma and Pa*, a quarter-hour serial drama.

Walter first worked with "Uncle Mort" Hal Peary on the February 7, 1937 episode of *Fibber McGee and Molly*, playing the bratty son of a traveling saleslady portrayed by Zasu Pitts.

And for Tetley, 1937 was the start of a whole new career.

THE BERGEN EVENING RECORD, MONDAY, APRIL 13, 1936.

RIDGEFIELD PARK YOUTH PORTRAYS FAMOUS CHARACTERS

"I can be tough. . . .   "and obstinate. . . .   "and so sweet."

alter Tetley of Ridgefield Park is the clever kid of radio. In 1935 the young star participated in more in 150 programs, including Show Boat, The New Penny starring Helen Hayes, The Lady Next Door, wn Hall Tonight. For versatility it's hard to find his equal. Walter has played on the air the boyhood pies of such contrasting personalities as Babe Ruth, Jack Dempsey, the Barrymores, Richard Barthelmess. Young Tetley, who is a boy of as many faces as roles, is shown above in a series of candid camera closeups.

Walter Tetley, prince of brat voices.

IX

WALTER HAD BEEN WORKING for Fred Allen more and more throughout 1936. Fred had been urging the little fellow to try his luck in films, but unless roles were certain and just as constant as radio work, Tetley's mother was hesitant about a switch to the West Coast. But when Fred got him a small unbilled appearance in his latest film, *Sally, Irene and Mary*, Walter felt his chances were good with a foot in the door.

So, after his usual morning appearance on *The Children's Hour*, the Tetleys began the long journey westward on Sunday, September 12, 1937. In between film auditions, Walter appeared in regular broadcasts on Allen's show from September 29 through December 29, 1937. He was a hit with his comic timing, and much beloved by Allen.

When the script called for it, Fred Allen always preferred Walter to any other "boy" voice. "Tet is a better actor than nine out of ten adults in radio," said Allen, "and he was just as good three years ago. That kid can do anything. The only reason he's not an English professor in Harvard right now is that radio pays better. When he plays my son in a skit, he mimics the voice perfectly in whatever accent I'm using. Chinese, Oxford, hillbilly, and he can do Scottish better than any of us.

"He bones up on his lines until he's letter perfect. He's actually got us in the habit of expecting so much from him that on a few occasions we've bawled him out for slight mistakes that we'd probably overlook in an adult. He cries like any sensitive kid does when you hurt his feelings, because of course he isn't the tough little brat he seems to be in some scripts—he wouldn't last fifteen minutes in this business if he was—and it's rather a shocking revelation after you've known him to discover he's just a child after all."

Walter suggested a few gags that worked their way into Wednesday night *Town Hall Tonight* broadcasts, and Allen urged the young man to write some sketches for the show. "But if I tried to do that," Walter said at the time, "I think I'd be overstepping myself."

Yet he was always proud of the show and being a part of the team called the Fred Allen Art Company: Minerva Pious, Lionel Standor, Eileen Douglas, Jack Smart, John Brown, and Walter Tetley. Fred Allen himself would often bring Tetley press notices—good ones—for Walter's scrapbook. "They don't mean I'm good," Walter admitted, "they just mean my press agent is earning his salary."

One enthusiastic review of a specific episode gave it three stars: "The high spot of the first half was the skit with Fred, Portland, and that amazing boy actor who spouts polysyllables with all the ease of a radio editor splitting an infinitive."

But Walter was the kind of person who paid more attention to the rare bad notices, concerned about what went wrong or why the press was getting it wrong. One reviewed called Walter rather flippant, to which Tetley responded, "I don't like that. It will lead people to believe I think a lot of myself, and that isn't true."

When Allen returned to New York, Tetley stayed. There was now too much film and radio work for him to switch coasts again. He was also doing bits in various advertising skits that interrupted programs.

Yet the public appearances still continued. One such big do was for the annual dance of Job's Daughters Hollywood Bethel. Jimmy Walsh and his orchestra led the entertainment that night at the Casino Gardens, with

Walter Tetley in "a humorous monologue," plus Nancy Welford (singer of *No, No, Nanette* fame), Mary Kay Harper, "novelty tap dancer," and, among others, Fox actress Dorothy Mayhew.

Both Tetley and his mother thought they would be better served launching Walter into a film career, now that he was known nationally as a "household voice." But though moving to California still meant a lot of good radio work, a career in pictures never seemed to materialize fully. Roles were limited mostly to bit parts such as bellhops and messengers, though his resume' did begin to rack up credits in some significant films.

The move West was also what ended the carefully preserved list of credits and scrapbooks that chronicled Walter's early career. It's hard to believe that Mrs. Tetley would not have come to Hollywood with Walter. So it's more than likely Walter's father had kept up the credit list, but unfortunately he could not move out of the East Coast due to his postal job. A few credits were typed or written in the notebook between September 29, 1937 and April 3, 1938, but not as many as before. Either Walter was too busy with breaking into films to do as much radio as

Walter (looking a little self-conscious) with his friends Mrs. and Mr. Wade, Jessie Campbell Tetley and her sister Anna Campbell, at a wedding reception.

Walter with friends: Mr. and Mrs. Wade, Edward Everett Horton and Wallace Ford.

before, or he or his mother did not have the time or inclination to keep the list updated; or both.

1938 was the start of Walter's film career. He first appeared in *Sally, Irene and Mary* with later radio co-star Alice Faye. The film was set to open at Grauman's Chinese Theatre on March 4, 1938 at which time Alice's and husband/co-star Tony Martin's feet were set in cement. But the event had to be postponed until March 20th since Alice fell ill.

Walter had a brief part in *A Trip to Paris*, but it was the follow up feature at MGM that brought Walter one of his most prestigious films: *Lord Jeff, or The Boy from Barnardos*. It was a veritable Who's Who of Hollywood young actors: Freddie Bartholomew, Mickey Rooney, Peter Lawford. Plus the big names of Charles Coburn, George Zucco, Gale Sondergaard and others. It was produced in Culver City, California by Frank Davis, with Sam Wood directing. Naturally, Tetley played a Scottish boy.

He then quickly reported to Republic Pictures for the part of the tough kid Mulligan in *Prairie Moon*, a western with Gene Autry. After

---

METRO-GOLDWYN-MAYER PICTURES
CULVER CITY

"LORD JEFF"
or
"The Boy From Barnardos"
Produced at Culver City, Cal., 1938

Cast	Played by:
Geoffrey Braemer	FREDDIE BARTHOLOMEW
Terry O'Mulvaney	MICKEY ROONEY
Capt. Briggs	CHARLES COBURN
Mrs. Briggs	EMMA DUNN
"Crusty" Jelks	HERBERT MUNDIN
John Cartwright	JOHN BURTON
Albert	TERRY KILBORNE
Benny	PETER LAWFORD
Tommy	WALTER TETLEY
Supt. Stepney Causeway	WALTER KINGSFORD
Mr. Burke	CHARLES COBURN
James Hampstead	GEORGE ZUCCO
Doris Clandon	GALE SONDERGAARD
Scott	MATTHEW BOULTON
Magistrate	
Producer FRANK DAVIS	Director SAM WOOD

completion of the film Walter joined the cowboy star for some personal appearances.

In 1939 Walter made six films. He had a brief bit with W.C. Fields (the man who couldn't stand children) in *You Can't Cheat an Honest Man*. He joined Boris Karloff as a chimney sweep in *The Tower of London*, one of many roles for which he received no screen credit.

Around 1939 a local paper from Tetley's own Bergen County proudly proclaimed "Walter Tetley is doing better than alright in Hollywood and he is not one of those blond effeminate screen lover types. He is famous for his voice. For the past three weeks he has been providing the voice for the title role in Disney's *Pinocchio*." In fact, he had only made a voice test for the role.

Prairie Moon, Republic Pictures, 1938. Tommy Ryan, David Gorcey and Walter Tetley.

The Spirit of Culver, Universal Pictures, 1939.

On the set of *The Spirit of Culver* at Universal Studios. Cast members Freddie Bartholomew, Jackie Cooper, Jackie Moran, Gene Reynolds and Tim Holt help Walter celebrate his 23rd birthday. 1938.

With an even larger salary from film and radio work, Walter was now living in a more spacious home at 744 North Gramercy Place in Hollywood. On March 9, 1939 he there received a telegram of thanks from Walter Wanger, chairman of the Hollywood branch of the Los Angeles Jewish Community Committee for his part in a radio program on the previous Monday night.

In that same year he appeared with Jackie Cooper, Freddie Bartholomew and Andy Devine in *Spirit of Culver*, directed by Joseph Santley, original screenplay by Whitney Bolton and Nathanael West.

There was a rumor, printed in *National Box Office Digest* on February 17, 1939 that studio executives had delayed the film's premiere in order to preview the retakes that had been made in order to beef up Walter's part. He played "Rocks," the comic role. During the filming of it at Universal Walter tried to organize a Scottish bagpipe band among the youngsters on the lot, in order to join Jackie Cooper's band in a concert. If he was ever able to gather up enough eclectic talent is open to speculation.

That was also the year 23-year-old Tetley played "Pee Wee" with Charles Powers, Johnny Fitzgerald and Anne Shirley in RKO's *Boy Slaves*. It was the powerful story of a group of kids who are besieged in a farmhouse and are threatened with killing by the brutal overseers of a turpentine

Boy Slaves, RKO, 1939. Walter is leaning against the building.

Boy Slaves, RKO, 1939.

camp from which they had escaped. The film was an impressive expose'
of the harsh exploitation of child labor in the early part of the 20th century.

Meantime, Walter was still doing live shows in his Scots persona.
On June 15, 1939 a Police Benefit show in Rialto, California featured
him in a production led by Frank Corbett in which "Pop-Eye the Sailor
man will appear at this performance with his company of actors." Other
"leading Broadway vaudeville acts" appeared "through the courtesy
of Arthur Fisher Agency," including Uncle Don of radio fame, and the
Wonder Dog! The musical director was Paul Scholz of Leo Feist Music
Publishers, with music for the acts and dancing by Bob Oakley and band.
A complete "picture show" was also part of the festivities, as well as prizes:
the lucky boy received a baseball autographed by Babe Ruth, and the lucky
girl, a Shirley Temple doll. Two shows were given.

During 1940 Walter appeared in six films, two of which were
uncredited. In *Emergency Squad*, directed by Edward Dmytryk, he played
Matt. He was also in *Framed*, which had to do with a young newspaper
reporter who finds himself framed for murder. It starred Frank Albertson
and Constance Moore. Walter was cast as Cadet Blackburn in *Military*

Let's Make Music, RKO, 1941, with Elizabeth Risdon and Joyce Compton.

Academy which starred Tommy Kelly and *Dead End* star Bobby Jordan. In *Under Texas Skies* he portrayed the tough kid Theodore who was forced into having his hair cut in one short comic relief scene in this western starring Robert Livingston and Bob Steele. In *The Villain Still Pursued Her* Walter was cast as yet another (telegram) delivery boy in this Buster Keaton sound feature. And in the musical *Let's Make Music*, Tetley, as Eddie the office boy, joined an eminent cast of Bob Crosby, Jean Rogers, Joyce Compton, Benny Rubin and more.

X

AFTER A SUCCESSION OF BIT PARTS in mostly minor films, Walter was ready for something more, a great challenge and more stability of work. When his life-changing radio series, *The Great Gildersleeve* came along, little Tetley was all set.

It was on *The Great Gildersleeve* that Walter achieved his greatest success. Hal Peary's Gildersleeve character had been popular enough on *Fibber McGee and Molly* to mark it as radio's first spin off series. After an audition show made for the Johnson Company (Fibber's sponsor) on May 14, 1941, the series premiered for Kraft Foods on August 31, 1941. Gildersleeve,

The great cast of *The Great Gildersleeve*.

affectionately shortened to 'Gildy' by one of the main characters, was a middle-aged windbag who loved to boast as much as he loved to sing. Amidst romancing the local southern belle and locking horns with Judge Hooker, Gildy found his time in Summerfield filled up with taking care of his orphaned niece, Marjorie, and nephew, Leroy, played by Walter Tetley.

Always-12-year-old Leroy was Walter's favorite role of his career. It wasn't long before his catchphrases—"What a character!" "Are you kiddin'?" "For corn's sake!"—were mimicked by his thousands of fans that wrote in weekly. Though Walter was at his most visible during the Gildy years, he still shied away from most personal publicity. He relished in using his new-found mega-stardom to help the many causes he still endowed with money or personal appearances. Nevertheless his private life was still kept strictly private.

Leroy was a positive role model for kids. He was the epitome of the ordinary boy who got into scrapes, let himself be talked into wild schemes for the sake of fun or money, but never gave his "Uncle Mort" (often just "Unk") any real, long-lasting trouble. The most exasperating "abuse" Gildy had to take was the constant deflating of the large man's ego, when Leroy would remind Gildy of the truth behind his boasts.

In 1976 Hal Peary recalled that a few years before the start of *Gildersleeve*, "Walter grew several inches after some treatment by a noted urologist here. I believe he was 22 at the time." Willard Waterman also remembered: "Walter's voice never changed, so he was able to play youngsters all of his life. He was about 5' 3" and had no facial hair, and his body was a little out of proportion. Nobody could get more out of a line than Walter." After the injections, Tetley shot up to around six feet tall.

Once Walter came on board the Gildersleeve series, his radio work ceased to be as prolific as it once was. Perhaps NBC wanted Tetley to be more associated with that role than anything else. Luckily the new-found fame led to roles, albeit small ones still, in more prominent films. In 1942 he held tiny roles in features such as *Eyes in the Night*, the entertaining mystery about a blind private detective with Edward Arnold in the lead. And *Thunder Birds*, a World War II movie that dealt with flight training at Thunderbird Field, Arizona. He was a mere messenger boy in that, but this was also the year of Tetley's biggest, and funniest role in a film.

In the Abbott and Costello vehicle *Who Done It?* Walter was only slated for a small part in one scene. But Lou Costello knew a good supporting player when he saw one, and kept requesting new scenes to be added for him. It was probably Tetley's largest screen role, and he was

Bud Abbott, Walter Tetley and Lou Costello in *Who Done It?*, Universal Studios, 1942.

a part of some of the best gags in the picture.

The film involved soda jerks (Bud and Lou) who really wanted to be radio writers: their own mystery series would star Muck and Mire. When they pose as detectives after a murder is committed, Abbott and Costello find themselves chased not only by the coppers, but by the killer as well (for a missing clue—a glove—that Costello had found).

It was a wartime plot which put Bud and Lou's pratfall and verbal comedy talents to perfect use. It also used Tetley's comic skills better than anything else outside of radio. One of the best gags was the counter scene in which the page boy (Tetley) bet the soda jerker (Lou) a nickel that he could drink orange juice faster than Lou could make it. The dopey jerk eagerly took the challenge, and won, gaining himself a whole nickel for the half dollar's worth of juice drunk. It was a wonderful scene that took ten takes to film. Unfortunately, Walter was allergic to citrus juices.

The scheming page boy had a crafty angle all through the movie. Early on he convinced Costello that Costello had yesterday's tickets for the radio show he wanted to see. When Costello threw his tickets away, Tetley calmly picked them up and escorted his lady friends in.

Another "cameo" came in *Pride of the Yankees*, the hit sentimental Gary Cooper baseball film. One reviewer wrote: "Clever fictionalizing and underplaying of the actual sport in contrast to the more human, domestic side of the great ballplayer make the film good box-office for all audiences, not forgetting the femmes." Tetley was seen as the uncredited cake delivery boy.

Walter was in good company for *Invisible Agent*, a 1942 wartime entry in the Universal horror series started by Claude Reins as the see-through villain in the original 1933 *Invisible Man*. This time Jon Hall is Frank Raymond, grandson of that original inventor, who is dropped into Germany to gather information from the bewildered Nazi leaders, played by arch-villains Peter Lorre and Sir Cedric Harwicke. It was a good war propaganda film to cheer for; unfortunately, Walter was again used in merely a small walk-on role.

In 1942's *Gorilla Man* Walter was in the film enough for his character to have a name. He was Sammy. The incredible plot involves Captain Craig Killian, played by John Loder, returning from a Continental raid with his British commandos. He has vital information, but is steered by Nazis to their private sanitarium so they can prevent him delivering the information. They discredit him with a few murders, but of course in the end he manages to round up the gang.

Typical of Hollywood, when *The Great Gildersleeve* had its own chance to shine as a film series, almost all of the elements—the cast—which made the radio show such a success were completely recast. The only exceptions were Harold Peary as Gildy and Lillian Randolph as Birdie. Margie was now played by Nancy Gates, and little Leroy had a real kid in the role for a change: Freddie Mercer.

The first film of the series, *The Great Gildersleeve*, received the most praise. Though the film was sorely lacking its Tetley support, *Variety* didn't seem to mind all of the substitutions. "Nancy Gates, a youngster, and Freddie Mercer, a ten-year-old lad, as Margie and Leroy, familiar characters of the radio shows, are neatly cast." It was released on January 2, 1943.

The series was followed by *Gildersleeve on Broadway*, *Gildersleeve's Bad Day*, and *Gildersleeve's Ghost*, all with Freddie Mercer featured in the Leroy role. Tetley did manage a bit part as a bellhop in *Gildersleeve on Broadway* in 1943. *Variety* couldn't stand the film, calling the story "a shoddy affair which bounces through a maze of stupid situations that are laughed at – rather than with."

But that was also the year Walter began lending his voice to Andy Panda cartoon shorts, as the lead character. The Walter Lantz creation began in 1939 for Universal Studios as a childlike, baby bear-type character. *Fish Fry*, Tetley's first of the series, was directed by Shamus Culhane. The plot involved Andy Panda buying a pet goldfish and trying to get it home before a hungry alley cat could do away with it. It was a cute character, and the seven-minute film was Oscar nominated for Best Short Subject. More Andy Panda cartoons followed through the 1940s, and were later repackaged for television in *The Woody Woodpecker Show* in 1957.

Radio was still keeping Tetley busy, however. During his Gildy years Walter found time to appear at times on *The Bob Burns Show* between February 18th and June 17, 1943. He also did guest shots on *The George Burns and Gracie Allen Show, Radio Almanac, Command Performance* and *Suspense*.

Tetley's dramatic abilities were ably showcased on *Suspense*. On December 13, 1943 he supported Cary Grant on an episode entitled "The Black Curtain"; on April 27, 1944 he returned with Gene Kelly in "Death Went Along for the Ride"; on November 16, 1944 with Robert Cummings in "Dead of Night"; on February 8, 1945 with Claire Trevor and Nancy Kelly in "Tale of Two Sisters"; and on August 8, 1946 he was heard with Cathy and Elliot Lewis in "Dead Ernest."

In February of 1947 he was heard in a supporting role on *The Alan Young Show*. Also in 1947 the Mutual Network began an anthology series, *Family Theater*, at the suggestion of a Catholic priest, Father Patrick Peyton, in an effort to promote family unity and prayer. Each week varying guest stars donated their services free of charge. Walter appeared a number of times. On July 24, 1947 he was heard on the episode "Brass Buttons," about a tough policeman, and on January 8, 1948 he returned in "The Happiest Person in the World" with William Bendix and Bea Benaderet. The role gave him a rare chance to display his many talents.

During 1944 he had a number of varying film roles. He was briefly seen in the musical *Bowery to Broadway* with Jack Oakie. He played a grocery boy in *Molly and Me*, starring the legendary Gracie Fields and Monty Woolley. He also appeared in the star-studded radio tribute, *Follow the Boys* with George Raft at the helm, in which Tetley appeared as a soldier. Though the films were good and somewhat high profile, with the roles being so thankless and miniscule, it was no wonder Walter was getting fed up with his "movie career." He preferred radio, and with good reason.

The Great Gildersleeve in rehearsal.

When *The Great Gildersleeve* series was at its height of popularity, Walter was receiving a lot of fan mail. So was "Leroy."

The "brat" once received a package containing the Van Court Scientific Course in Boxing to protect himself from his overbearing uncle, so believable was Tetley's performance.

During the series Walter lived with his family fifteen minutes out of Hollywood in San Fernando Valley. There, at the place they named "Big Oak Ranch," they had room for their small farm and stable with two horses, one of which pulled an old-fashioned "surrey with the fringe on top" (and had been used in many films). Also around the spread could be found four dogs, five cats, two hundred chickens and two ducks, which Walter named Hedy and Lana.

The home itself was an attractive white stucco Spanish-style house built around a big oak tree "whose branches afford a natural cooling system." It was Walter's haven away from the rush of Hollywood work, where he could lounge around his swimming pool with his father who seemed to spend all his time there. His mother was then a Lieutenant Colonel in the Women's Emergency Corps and was in charge of a free canteen for servicemen in Beverly Hills. His brother was a precision parts inspector in a nearby defense plant.

Angus Campbell states, "I grew up in the Walter Tetley home that my parents purchased in 1955 in Encino, California, at 17357 Magnolia Blvd. It was the most wonderful of places to grow up, with a huge oak tree that the house was built around (which has since died and the house has been completely remodeled… very ugly now). We were told the family just wanted to get out of the house quickly due to deaths (his parents?). A baby grand piano was left behind, as well as many old leather bound books, oriental rugs, and old stage actor photos (such as Lillian Russell, signed).

"There were many outbuildings on the 1.3 acre property and I always wondered what the full use of them was for. There was a theater he built which he called 'The Spotlight Theater.' I still have the sign from the entrance door. I would love to know the history… he must have put on plays. There was a ticket window on the side of the building and a bar inside for refreshments. We used the building as storage for hay for our horses! There was a corral, and he must have raised dogs because there was a dog run as well.

"Many old time actors lived in the area at the time… such as Edward Everett Horton. So I wonder if they all had grand old times putting on shows for the locals. I also learned through reading newspaper clippings that he would have the Boys Club kids come down during the summer to swim in the pool on Tuesdays or Thursdays. I believe he was a very good and decent person and I would love to learn more information about him. A bit of a mystery, however, was when we put new wallpaper up in my bedroom… we found uncashed checks stuffed in a hole in the wall! My mother thought they may have been poker debts he refused payment on."

XI

THOUGH WALTER APPEARED IN SIX FILMS in 1944, his movie career was clearly winding down. He played a mere call boy in the Jack the Ripper thriller, *The Lodger*, starring Laird Cregar, George Sanders and Merle Oberon. Also, he had a bit part in *Her Primitive Man* with Louise Allbritton. He could be seen briefly as the florist's assistant in *Casanova Brown*, starring Gary Cooper.

He was only an uncredited messenger (again) in *Pin Up Girl*, but it was a Technicolor musical with plenty of splash and lots of Betty Grable. *Variety* wrote, "This is one of those escapist film musicals which you accept, or else. It makes no pretenses at ultra-realism, and if you get into the mood fast that it's something to occupy your attention for an hour and a half, it's all very pleasing and pleasant." Joe E. Brown and Martha Raye provided the comic support, while Mark Gordon and James Monaco supplied some catchy songs via "Time Alone Will Tell," "Red Robins, Bob White and Blue Birds," and others. At least Tetley's cameos were in popular features.

Walter didn't fare much better the following year in a walk-on role in Fred Allen's *It's in the Bag*. It's one of many cameos that dots the "revue" picture in which Allen inherits a load of cash but it gets sewn into the lining of a chair. The chairs are of course scattered all over – from Jack Benny's apartment to a restaurant filled with singing waiters (Rudy Vallee, Don Ameche and Victor Moore). It was a fun film, filled with gags and appearances from Allen's Alley people. Unfortunately, the critics weren't kind to the idea. *Variety* stated, "This rat's nest of nonsense defies the sober description of a rational mind." But for those fans who enjoyed the steady stream of guests on Allen's radio show, it was a rather delightful collection of pearls strung together. It was just unfortunate that, as usual, Walter Tetley was given almost nothing to do.

His last screen appearance was with Bert Gordon, better known to radio audiences as The Mad Russian, in *How Do You Do?*, released in 1946. It didn't do very well at the box office.

Foolin' for the camera.

Except for a few more Andy Panda cartoons, Walter gave up films in favor of his more substantial radio work.

In 1947 he was signed for a leading role in a syndicated, transcribed domestic comedy, *The Anderson Family*.

Finally, on April 10, 1948 Walter was the closest he would ever come to a starring role when he auditioned for NBC's *The Kid on the Corner*, which was never picked up by a sponsor. Tetley was to have been a tough newsboy who got into trouble around his neighborhood. Harry Von Zell played straight man to his wise-cracking antics. When interest failed in the series, so did Walter's hopes of ever finding himself as anything but a supporting player.

But this was probably for the best, and most likely what he wanted. Starring in a series meant more attention, more interviews, less privacy. Tetley, set in his ways, did not want the limelight shinning on him, especially as he got older. He was the humble sort who enjoyed his work, but when the microphone was turned off and the applause died down, he preferred to leave it all behind, and simply "go home." This same attitude may have made it easier when he eventually left the business.

Ira Cochin, one of Walter's friends after World War II, explains: "Walter Tetley was born in 1915. When I met him in 1945, he was 30 years old. If you stood close to him, you could not detect the slightest indication of a beard—not even peach fuzz. His face was as smooth as that of a child. He was 'child' personified. And he sustained all these features till he was 40 years old! He was literally the Fountain of Youth.

"I met this talented man in an Army hospital in 1945 during WWII. As a soldier when I was 20, I had lost an eye. For the healing and rehabilitation process, I remained in the Army as a patient at Birmingham General Hospital in Van Nuys, California, a suburb of Los Angeles. It was a very long stay, and for diversion, I became involved in the hospital radio broadcasting system. The soldier patients broadcast a radio show twice a week. Since this was radio, without a studio audience, no one saw the performers, permitting them to read scripts, obviating the need to memorize the dialog. Various Hollywood actors and actresses volunteered to perform, and in return, our radio broadcast provided a vehicle to showcase their talents. It was of mutual benefit, a pleasant activity that provided camaraderie and fun for us all.

"When WWII ended and peace was declared, servicemen waiting for discharge could get permission from the Army Commander to be employed part time by civilian firms. Sterling Holloway had arranged for me to be interviewed and I was hired as a freelance scriptwriter for *The Great Gildersleeve* radio show, and I had the job till I was discharged. But my real task was to act as liaison for Walter Tetley, and to work with him at his home in Encino, another suburb of Los Angeles.

"Sterling had said, 'Tell me something; did you get along with kids your own age?' I was embarrassed and replied, 'No. That's the down side of my ability to converse with people who were so much older than I. Kids my age shunned me, and thought I was very odd.' Sterling pursed his lips and said, 'Let me tell you why I asked. There's an actor who bears the same affliction.' I interrupted, 'Affliction? No, that's my asset.' Sterling insisted, 'Yes, affliction. The actor I'm thinking of plays the role of Leroy on a radio show called *The Great Gildersleeve*. He got the part because he looks like a child. That's his gift. But he must deal with adults. That's his affliction. I'm sure he could use you as his liaison.' I chuckled, 'Well, maybe when I get discharged a year from now.' 'No, he could use you now.' He pondered a while. 'Can't you get a furlough? Never mind, let me find a way.'

"Walter's brother volunteered to pick me up at my Military Post, and as he drove, he asked me why I didn't drive. I explained that I had lost an eye in service, and that I had not yet learned how to judge distance. So I was a potential hazard on the road. However, I was studying to be an engineer. We arrived at a small ranch, about 120 by 250 feet in the shape of the state of Nevada. It had a huge ranch-type house with built-in garage, a stable with two horses, and a sizable built-in swimming pool (which was quite uncommon at that time). This was Walter Tetley's home.

"Noting my Army uniform, Walter asked me to sign his guest register. He had always wanted to befriend a real soldier, and he treated me like a celebrity. He wanted to show me around the place, but his brother interrupted to tell him that I had lost one eye and was a wounded soldier. Walter immediately got me a chair, and he asked if I wanted something cool to drink. As I walked about, he ran ahead to move things out of my way. It was obvious that Walter was very sensitive to a handicapped person's needs. I knew he wasn't a child, but it certainly was a notable revelation to learn that the actor who played the role of ten-year-old Leroy was a thirty-year-old man. He was neither a midget nor a dwarf. He was

Tetley and friends at The Cocoanut Grove club in Los Angeles.

a perfectly formed undersized man with a child's voice, appearance, and mannerisms—with a round cherubic face.

"Walter and I sat poolside and we had a long conversation about showbiz. We laughed at the notion that silent movies had no sound, and that radio had no picture. We rehashed a number of the old movies and old radio shows. Then he said, 'I wondered what a radio show would be like if the audience could see the actors on stage. But then they couldn't be allowed to read scripts. It would be like a movie.' He scrunched up his mouth. 'That wouldn't be any good. Radio would then be the same as movies.' He thought about that for a moment. 'Movies. I was in movies. And I appeared in movies with famous stars.' I asked how he felt about working with celebrities. 'Being on the same sound stage with an actor that I had seen in movies was a tremendous boost for my morale. It made me want to do movies forever. But later, I changed my mind and preferred radio. But I still was in about 50 movies—bit parts, and I was told, "There's no bit parts—only bit actors." Nice phrase, but I still continued to call them bit parts.' I asked, 'How do you feel about *The Great Gildersleeve* show?' He huffed, 'Well that sure isn't a bit part. How do I feel? I know I'm somebody. I just wish I could make friends with the cast. I sometimes feel like an outsider.'

"I asked, 'Do you like reading a script instead of memorizing it?' Walter tilted his head in thought. 'I never had trouble memorizing, but with a script I can do more with my voice. And in movies I never had such a large part. On this show, I don't feel limited.' I explained, 'That's because the show is a departure from comedy show history.' 'How do you mean?' I sat back and shrugged, 'In the theatrical past, comedy shows consisted of a group of unrelated comic sketches—not one overall plot like a book, play or movie. The objective of such comedy shows in the past was merely a collection of jokes.' He said, 'I never noticed, but thinking back, I used to listen to all the comedy shows, and you're right. Yes, a lot of short skits.' He thought a while. 'But I thought there was a few that had a story for the whole hour. What about the Marx Brothers? And Cary Grant?' I smiled, 'Those were movies.' He chuckled, 'Let me think. There must be one that had a story for the full hour.' He pondered a while and said, 'OK, I give up. What's the name of a show that had all one story?' I replied, 'This wasn't a riddle or a puzzle. The reason you can't think of one is because there were no comedy shows like that.' He wrinkled his brow. 'I wonder why.'

"I pondered, *How deep can I go? Walter certainly is following me.* I decided to proceed: 'Hmmm. There never was a show like that in the past. But there is one now. It's called *The Great Gildersleeve* show.' He was a bit annoyed. 'Hey, that ain't fair. I'm in that show. Now that you mention it, yes, but how come?' I said, 'Your show is a pioneer in the world of comedy. It has a single story, where each scene advances the plot, as it does in a book, play or movie. That demands a lot from the writers, and performers. And you are doing wonderfully.' He grinned broadly. 'Really? And they do give me the lead in some of the shows.' I chuckled, 'They're businessmen, and they know you draw an audience. And the people who pay for the ads also like that.' Walter scratched his head. 'You and I have been talking grown up stuff. Thanks.' I was stunned. Had no one ever spoken to Walter Tetley as an adult?

"Walter's brother came over to us and said, 'I figured that since you were an engineer, could you assemble and install an electrified trap for insects?' I replied, 'Sure, it's the least I can do to repay you for giving me a ride.' It was a metal structure about 3 feet long, and 4 by 4 inches across. I worked well into the night before the job was completed. I tested the trap, and when a bug entered it, I heard the *snap* sound of the spark. Yuck. It was quite late, and I was ready to return to the Army Post. 'Army Post!' I yelped and froze. 'I forgot to report in to the Army Post before curfew.' Walter calmly told me, 'I could tell you were going to be busy a long time. So, I phoned the Commander at your Army Post and notified him of your predicament. I hope you don't mind, but I kind of emphasized that you were half blind and could not make it back before curfew. He said OK, and he signed you in.' I was stunned by the thoughtfulness of this guy. He knew exactly what to do on my behalf. This certainly was not the behavior of a child. Walter said. 'You don't want to be traveling at night. You can sleep here.' Then he and his brother set up the guest room for me, and I slept well that night.

"The next morning, I didn't have to travel to Walter's home. I was there already. Walter and I began our teamwork. As Walter's liaison, one of my tasks was to write comedy material, and another job was to listen to Walter read his lines. While he didn't have the natural style of a comedian, a humorous script made him a great comedian, for several reasons. One, he read the lines with perfection. Two, he knew how to add just the right sparkle to his youthful voice. Three, he knew when to pause and how long. He really was the writer's ideal model of an actor. He fully understood the script and never misread a part. It was Walter's prerogative to decide whether we'd work all day or a half, how many days a week, and this changed as he saw fit. It was a bit startling for a guy who looked like a child to be so adult in his work habits. He was 10 years older than I was. I noticed that he never had any friends and we talked freely about it. The problem was that he looked, spoke, and acted like Leroy, the child he played. So adults were not drawn into friendship with him. And 10-year-old kids could not identify with him, since mentally he was a full-grown man. This was the down side of his non-aging features. I became acutely aware that he must have had long bouts with loneliness.

"This dichotomy also permeated his relations with his own family. I noticed that his brother and parents treated him like the ten-year-old he played. He had to ask his mother if he could go for a swim, to eat a snack before lunch, and to take something out of the garage. I'll admit that I was shocked, but figured it was best not to interfere. Walter's family life was outside the jurisdiction of my job as his liaison. I felt empathy with him and I was able to help him, for I had lived the same dichotomy that he did. Walter and I were soul mates.

"As a momentary break from the strict and tedious routine, Walter invited me to ride one of his horses, and he took a photo of me in the saddle. However, he was loath to allow me to take his picture. This was the first time that I had witnessed his objection to a photo. He was also loath to write a letter or to sign his name. Only a few photos of Walter are available to the public. Consequently, many people in the theater business never saw Walter. They were not sure what he looked like. They imagined that he might be short. They figured he made his voice high pitched for effect.

"Walter and I were getting to know one another. We talked about what he'd do when he grew up. This was his dilemma. He was thirty-years old, and he was grown up. There was little I could offer as advice, because I never had any training as a guidance counselor. The best I could do was to listen to what he had to say, and encourage him to follow his ideals. He needed to be revered as an adult—and he deserved that honor.

"One time, Walter was down in the dumps. It was his volition to call it a day and send me home. But that would only leave him feeling blue. As a comedian I had an idea. 'Say Walter, how about some hot chocolate and cookies?' The little boy in him was delighted. I spoke like a professor, 'But it tastes best if made with cold water. Now, I offer the appropriate warning. Since the cold water tap is on the right hand side, never turn it on with your left hand. Because you must cross the plumbing fixture.' As I said that, the spigot slid up my sleeve. And when I turned on the water, we had Niagara Falls in the kitchen. The water poured out of my sleeve into the sink, which was okay. But it also gushed out of the neck of my shirt. Since I wasn't a fish, I was drowning. The scene was so funny that Walter convulsed with laughter. By the time his guffaw died down, I had heated the drink and served it.

"But Walter wasn't able to let go of the gag. Seeing the water dripping from my sleeve as I reached for a cookie, he suddenly burst out laughing. And it was a burst of monumental proportions. But his mouth was closed and the warm chocolate drink poured out of his nose. That sent him into more convulsions of laughter. Of course, his laugher was contagious, and I had no control. Did you ever laugh so hard and so long that your jaws ached? He was over the blues, and we resumed working on the script.

"One day, Walter and I finished early and I planned to take him to a local movie theater. We got popcorn, hot dogs, and soda. However, the theater manager wouldn't allow us to bring food into the theater. We left in a huff, but I was undaunted and made plans of retaliation. And I had drafted Walter into the mischievous plot. I don't know if Walter ever did anything mischievous before this time. If he didn't, then I was a bad influence. Nevertheless, Walter felt driven to be my accomplice. Either that, or perhaps he was laughing too hard to object. We took a taxi to a department store and we bought a child-size rag doll. We removed some of the stuffing, and filled it with the food. Walter was of little help as he was laughing the whole time.

"We entered the theater. The ticket booth was in the lobby, which was dimly lit. That was to our advantage. Walter and I began to 'walk' the doll to make her look like a real child, and we bought her a ticket to enter the theater. It was a hilarious adventure, and I was afraid that Walter's high-pitched cackle would get us thrown out of the theater. But a very funny movie with Fred MacMurray was playing, and no one noticed us. Walter was still laughing as we watched the movie and ate our contraband food. Walter never laughed so much in his life. It did my heart good to see the guy in such a state of hilarity.

"In May of 1946, it was a sad moment when I received my travel orders for my military discharge in Sacramento, California. It was time for me to return home—and to leave the West coast. Walter insisted on taking me to the train station. When we got into a cab, he explained another woe. Because he looked like a child, he wasn't allowed to get a driver's license. As we rode, a thought hit me. I hoped that I had started him along the avenue toward self-esteem. He still had no friends, and he still was reluctant to write letters and sign his name. But he no longer asked for his mother's permission to go for a swim, to have a snack before lunch, or to take something out of the garage. And he made sure people listened to him. He was beginning to know who he was, and that he rated the status of adulthood. I simply talked to him like the grown-up he was, and listened to him as an equal."

XII

IN 1948–OCTOBER 3RD TO BE EXACT—Walter began his second most famous role: that of the insufferable, loud mouth delivery boy, Julius Abbruzio on *The Phil Harris/Alice Faye Show*. Sporting a semi-Brooklyn accent, Julius was almost the exact opposite of the good-natured Leroy. The impish lad delighted in causing trouble, playing jokes and generally giving it to Phil and Remley good.

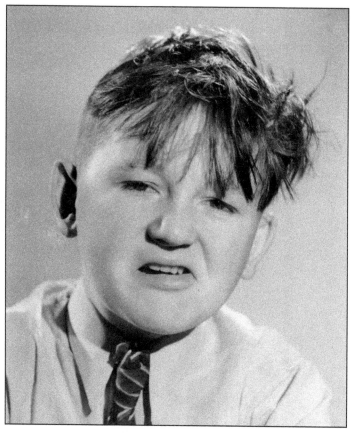

No one played the brat better than Tetley.

The Harris-Faye series was sort of a spin-off *of The Jack Benny Program*, with Phil and Alice playing themselves, taking the character Frankie Remley (noted for being drunk all the time on Jack's show) into their world. Many of the plots were like *The Flintstones/ Honeymooners*, involving Phil and Frankie's wild exploits. Rexall Drugs sponsored the show which cost $14,500 a week to produce.

Walter usually emerged in the second half of the half-hour program, when the boys were already in hot water. Julius had a few cute catch phrases to shout back at them: a Leroy-type "Are you kiddin'?" and the more New York-oriented "Get outta here!" The audience ate it up.

It must have felt like old home week when Fred Allen visited the January 23, 1949 program. Though Walter had no scenes with Fred, the two traded stories and caught up on old times before and after the show. The following excerpt from that episode is typical of Tetley's role in the fun. Julius would start out as a wise guy, relishing in taunting Harris and Remley about whatever they were getting themselves into that week. But as the comedy increased, the worm, and tables, slowly turned on the poor little delivery boy:

Bowling with Alice Faye and friends.

HARRIS: It's no use, Frankie, this suit of Willie's doesn't fit me.

FRANKIE: I don't know. You got it on, didn't you?

HARRIS: Just barely. It's too tight. Look at the way these pants cling to my legs. How does it look, Remley?

FRANKIE: Very alluring. It looks like black underwear.

HARRIS: Well, I don't care how it looks. I got my heart set on that Ball and I'm going. And now that we found Willie's invitation you can go too.

FRANKIE: Yeah, I—(TAKE) Hey, wait a minute. I just happened to think, I haven't got a full dress suit either.

HARRIS: Where can we get one for you?

FRANKIE: I don't know, but I'll get one if I have to go through every transom in this hotel.

SOUND: DOOR OPENS

FRANKIE: Come on. Curly, I'm in a hurry, move faster.

HARRIS: I can't. This dress suit of Willie's is choking me, all over. If I make a sudden move I'll split it.

FRANKIE: Well, stop waddling. You look ridicu…

TETLEY: Hiya, Mr. Remley, I…Hey, Mr. Remley, where you going with that penguin?

HARRIS: I ain't no penguin, Julius.

TELTEY: Oh it's Mr. Harris. What are you made up for?

HARRIS: I'm going to the President's Ball and this is my full dress suit.

TETLEY: This is a full dress suit?

HARRIS: Yeah. How do I look, kid?

TETLEY: (LAUGHS) Oh brudder, are you bow legged.

FRANKIE: Curly ain't bow legged. He just happens to have a well-turned ankle, all the way up to the knee.

HARRIS: Well, maybe I'm a *little* bow legged.

TETLEY: A *little*? You look like you're standing on a pair of ice tongs.

HARRIS: You got a lot of nerve making fun of me. You look a little baggy yourself. What have you got on under that overcoat?

TETLEY: My full dress suit. My Uncle Herman got me an invitation to the Ball.

FRANKIE: You're wearing a full dress suit?–Curly, what do you think?

HARRIS: It's a little short but if you walk on your knees I think you can make it.

FRANKIE: Right. Julius, stand still.

TETLEY: Hey you guys, quit measuring me.

FRANKIE: Hold still. Think we can get away with this, Curly?

HARRIS: (SING SONG) We can try.

FRANKIE: (SING SONG) Let's get started.

TETLEY: (SING SONG) Over my dead body... Oh, oh, I shouldn't have said that.

HARRIS: Grab him, Frankie!

FRANKIE: Got him!

TETLEY: Get your paws offa me, you guys!

HARRIS: Quiet! A little slow music Remley, while I disrobe
           him. (FRANKIE SINGS "A PRETTY GIRL")

TETLEY: (YELLS) Stop taking my coat off. Let go of me! Gimme
           back my pants! Help! Help! Clothes-nappers!

But often Julius would get the better of Phil and his chum:

JULIUS: When you left town I didn't think they'd let you back
           in this country.

PHIL: Why?

JULIUS: Because it's against the law to smuggle dope across
           the border.

The beloved series ran through June 18, 1954.

    At some point Walter appeared briefly with an all-star radio cast on
the 3-album set, A Christmas Carol, for Columbia Records.

Scrooge:	Basil Rathbone
Fred:	Elliott Lewis
Bob Cratchet:	Jay Novello
Marley's Ghost:	Arthur Q. Bryan
Christmas Past:	Francis X. Bushman
Scrooge as a Boy:	Tommy Cook
Little Fan:	Rhoda Williams
Christmas Present:	Stuart Robertson
Mrs. Cratchet:	Paula Winslowe
Peter:	Dix Davis
Martha:	Lurene Tuttle

Tiny Tim:	Tommy Cook
Boy:	
1st Man:	Arthur Q. Bryan
2nd Man:	Stuart Robertson
Charwoman:	Paula Winslowe
Undertaker's Man:	Raymond Lawrence
Boy:	Walter Tetley
Narrator:	Harlow Wilcox

Between two hit series, the occasional guest shot and personal appearances, Walter showed no signs of slowing down, even though radio's days were numbered. On October 18, 1949 Walter made one of his rare television appearances, as guest on Joe Graydon's show over KLAC-TV at 9:30 p.m. Three days later Tetley called the square dance given at the Woodland Hills Community Center. He stomped his foot to the fiddle from 8 to 11 p.m. and had a ball, especially since he knew the event benefited the newly opened Woodland Hills Co-operative Nursery. Again, he gave his services freely. According to other accounts, it wasn't the first or last time he led that square dance.

Both of Walter's main radio series had a featured spot in the Santa Claus Lane Parade of Stars in Hollywood on November 16, 1949. It was led by the Phil Harris family, with the cast of *The Great Gildersleeve*, including Hal Peary, Marylee Robb and Walter, following on later.

As of Christmas Eve of that year Walter was a civic leader in San Fernando Valley, belonged to the Chamber of Commerce, was a member of the San Fernando Valley Boy Scouts' executive council, was associate Scout master for a troop of handicapped boys (Rainbow Troop #1260), and was honorary president of the Metropolitan Soccer League.

On January 25, 1950 Phil and the entire cast headed to New York to begin work on the March of Dimes campaign. They taped their January 29, February 5 and 12 shows from New York, and headed back to California for the February 19 program.

The *Citizen News* from Hollywood reported on February 24, 1950 that starting on March 25th Walter would be conducting "a dramatic school in his barn." It may have been for his Boy Scout troop which he would oversee until the end of his life.

In a way, Walter Tetley's showbiz career ended with radio's end. *The Great Gildersleeve* ended its long, prestigious run on March 21, 1957, finally losing the long battle against television. Many of radio's top voices either migrated to television or cartoon work. Walter did too, to a limited extent.

In 1956 he was hired by UPA to supply a voice in the *Gerald McBoing-Boing* TV series, in episodes of *Dusty of the Circus*. The series was later syndicated as part of *Mister Magoo and Friends*. Bill Scott, later of Bullwinkle fame (voicing Peabody to Walter's Sherman), was assistant producer on the show.

During the months of July through October 1957 Walter was heard briefly on *The Stan Freberg Show*, a summer replacement show for Jack Benny, and the last network comedy series on radio. Four years later Freberg underused Tetley again on his classic comedy album, *Stan Freberg Presents the United States of America Vol. 1*. He had a few lines in the Midnight Ride of Paul Revere and the discovery of electricity sketches.

An older and wiser Walter Tetley.

It must have been hard for a workhouse like Tetley to adapt to a sudden loss of definite, incessant employment. It was not a happy time. According to Hal Peary, Walter's parents and the brother he lived with passed away sometime in the 1950s. Edward Everett Horton, another famous voice from *Rocky and Bullwinkle*, lived nearby. But it's difficult to say if he had any close friends to which he could confide his troubles.

Around this time Walter was presented with an award from the Hollywood Coordinating Council "for his outstanding personal service to handicapped and underprivileged children," mainly for organizing Boy Scout Troop 1260. This troop was comprised entirely of shut-ins who were unable to participate in regular scouting activities. He began a local radio program aimed at his Scouts so they could "meet" right in the homes of the boys who otherwise could not get out. He would also invite the Boy Scouts to his ranch in the San Fernando Valley where they would lounge around the pool, play with his prize-winning cocker spaniels and enjoy a home away from home.

Whether or not Walter had been a Boy Scout himself is open to question. It's doubtful that he had had the time for such normal activities in his youth, since his mother took him from one radio or public

Pantomime Quiz, with Jimmy Lydon, Walter Tetley, Keefe Brasselle, Beverly Tyler, Mike Stokey (host, with fish), Adele Jergens, Hans Conreid, Robert Stack and Frank DeVol. Early 1950s.

appearance to another *constantly*. Perhaps in later life, free from the push of his mother, he felt he could give other boys, who also never had a chance at an "ordinary" life, what he had always missed.

As the Gildersleeve and Phil Harris programs came to an end in the 1950s, Walter had more time on his hands than in previous years.

He began to take refuge in an extra business pursuit. He ran a pet shop called The Happy Tail on Ventura Boulevard, inspired by his great interest and love of dogs. When the store originated, or how long it, continued is uncertain.

One of Tetley's few live television appearances came between 1949 and 1952 on *Pantomime Quiz*, which began as a local show in Los Angeles in 1948. The game show consisted of two teams of four celebrities each playing charades (subjects suggested by the viewers at home), guessing a famous phrase, quote, title, etc. within the two-minute time limit.

Hal Peary and Walter last worked together at a special Radio Night produced by Frank DeVol at the Hollywood Bowl in 1966. According to Peary, Walter "wow'd 'em as 'Leroy' and he had grown to nearly six feet at that time. Rather amazing! Walter's personal voice did change through the years but to quote him: 'I can still do Leroy. All I have to do is raise my eyebrows.'"

XIII

PERHAPS WALTER'S MOST ENDURING vocal performance was that of Sherman, Mr. Peabody's pet boy in the *Mr. Peabody's Improbable History* segments of *Rocky and His Friends*. Bill Scott, voice of Bullwinkle, Fearless Leader, Dudley Do-Right and others, projected his precise, Clifton Webb-type speech as lead dog Peabody, a pedantic white beagle who always wore a small red bow tie and thick spectacles.

Walter, of course, did his Leroy voice for the freckled, bespectacled, innocent little cartoon boy, Sherman.

Created by Ted Key (famous as the artist-creator of Hazel), the pun-filled cartoons began in 1959. The crudely-drawn Jay Ward animation had brilliant scripts (mostly written by Chris Hayward) of dog and boy meeting everyone from Napoleon to Confucius to Tom Thumb. They would time travel via the Wayback Machine to correct any history that was veering off the correct path towards catastrophe; the adventures would usually end in a pun bad enough to crack Sherman's thick glasses.

Before the famous and well-defined characters became Peabody and Sherman, the segment had been called *Danny Daydream*. Creator Ted Key explained: "Day dreaming is just another way to travel. You can go anywhere in the world, meet anyone who ever lived, invent, explore, party, fight, love, conquer, achieve, without spending a dime. It's a short cut to adventure, and thrills. A quick way to get out of the house. And if you're doing it on TV, as a kid named Danny, you can take your whole audience with you. Kids like yourself, or adults who are, in heart, still kids.

"But just being Danny Daydream wasn't enough. The 'concept' needed a 'kicker.' A fresh slant – so I gave him a take-charge companion. Daydream was an underlying concept, not a name, and too obvious. Time travel, not daydreaming, was introduced. Lists of names submitted. Names chosen. The 'people,' and 'events,' to 'got to.' I was delighted with the 'characters' they finally went with. I established the 'characters,' but Jay

Ward and his brilliant, inventive staff chose their 'missions.' They brought them to life, and I was pleased with the way they did it. More than pleased. Happy, and supportive. I thought Walter Tetley's voice was perfect for Sherman. Bill Scott and Jay Ward made the right choices. They didn't submit tests of Walter to me; nor of any of the voices. But the choices they did make were perfect.

"Years have passed since the show first took a bow. I was as delighted with it then as I still am now.

"It's my feeling that if there had been no 'Peabody and Sherman' segment, the Rocky and Bullwinkle Show would not have been on TV at all. It might not have been bought.

"My reasoning:

"Jay Ward came East, to New York City, with a five minute pilot of the Rocky and Bullwinkle show. The ad agency and sponsor liked it. 'What're you going to do with the other 25 minutes?' they asked Jay. He didn't

know. He didn't have the money for a longer pilot or another 'segment' to add to his *five minute* show.

"He became ill. He asked me if I could come up with something. I said, 'I'll try, Jay.' He flew back to the West Coast. Had a nervous breakdown, after turning over the project to my brother. (We were all neighbors and friends in Berkeley, California.) Somehow money was raised for the Peabody and Sherman pilot. The advertising agency *loved* it, and based on that discussion, decided to go ahead with the *whole half hour project*. Jay found Bill Scott to build up his West Coast studio and the show was on its way."

The first show, in which they met Ben Franklin, told the origin of boy and dog getting together: Peabody cast off his professorial guise for a moment to bark at the bullies beating up poor Sherman in an alley. Grateful, the little kid followed the dog home.

Tetley voiced all ninety-one 4.5 minute episodes of *Mr. Peabody's Improbable History*, which still remains one of the best components of *Rocky and His Friends*.

When the Golden LP, *Rocky and His Friends*, was released in 1960, Tetley/Sherman was given a solo number to sing. "I Wanna Go Back with the WABAC Machine" was a fun little novelty number harkening Tetley back to his vaudeville days.

On February 15, 1970 Hal Peary wrote to a fan:

"Walter Tetley, who played 'LEROY' for many years on the radio series, even with Waterman, is hospitalized at the Los Angeles County U.S.C. Medical Center, Ward 3700, 1200 N. State St., Los Angeles, Calif. 90033. Tetley was injured while riding a motorcycle—has two broken legs, two broken arms and a fractured pelvis. He will be there for at least two more months."

Early in 1970 while riding his motorcycle near Van Nuys, Walter was struck head-on by a motorist who failed to stop for a traffic light. He suffered internal injuries that put him in pain for the rest of his life.

On February 26, 1970 Peary wrote again to the fan: "Thanks for writing to Walter Tetley and for your trouble in asking others to do so. I know that he will enjoy all the communications. He is pretty lonely in that plaster of paris underwear and the pulleys..."

In April Walter was moved to Olive View Hospital, Ward 301, at 14701 Foothill Boulevard in Los Angeles County. He was there for at least 3 months.

Ailing though he was, Walter still wanted to work, and was grateful for the few opportunities that came his way. Don Pitts, his last agent, remembered the sad situation.

"When I got in the business, I looked him up. I was always his fan. But he didn't want to do anything at all. He was working in a pet shop in the Valley someplace. I talked him into coming in. He had no money. He ended up in Olive View Hospital and his insurance at SAG had run out, so he was destitute.

"I submitted him to Hanna-Barbera one day, for a kid's part, submitted him to Alex Loathy who had been out there forever, so I certainly assumed he knew who the hell Walter Tetley was. I brought in a tape I had Walter make, just before his accident. I played the tape, and Alex said, 'Yeah, he looks kinda like what I'm looking for.' So I set up the interview, but Walter was still in the hospital, so they were going to take him in an ambulance to the interview. He told the hospital if he could get this job, it could be applied against his bill. After the audition, Alex called from Hanna-Barbera and he was furious with me. 'How could you do this to me?' he shouted. I said, 'What are you talking about? Didn't he show up?' He said, 'I've never been so embarrassed in my whole life.

A mature, long-legged Walter relaxes at home.

I thought this was a kid! I was told he was in the lobby so I ran out there and here was this old man in a wheel chair with his leg up in a cast and a couple of attendants in white outfits standing with him. I said to the receptionist, "Where is Mrs. Tetley and her son?'" I asked, 'Well, how did he sound?' Alex said he sounded fine, just like the tape, but no, he wanted a kid!

"Alex said he wanted some tapes of other kids, and I gave him one of my son, who ended up getting the job. I felt so badly I told Walter the story, and he said, 'My whole life has been like that, Don. Once they saw me, I never got the job.'

"Walter said, 'They used to have a little suit for me over at Western Costume. It was a bellboy's suit, and whenever they had a bellboy's role in a feature film, they would just call over and get the suit, and I would get the call. But when the business changed, and they saw me, they just wouldn't hire me.' It was a very sad story. He was a super nice guy. A wonderful talent.

"When I was looking for him originally, everyone referred to him as 'little Walter.' When he came into the office to work with me, he was full grown. But unfortunately he had a very yellow, like jaundice, complexion. Very, very leathery looking skin, with these deep wrinkles in his skin. I'm sure it was all part of his condition."

His yellow leathery skin may have had to do with the hormone shots he took years earlier to cure his growth problem. Even Stan Freberg commented on Walter's sickly complexion when he worked with him on *Stan Freberg Presents The United States of America Vol. 1*:

"He was a wonderful guy. He was supposed to be a little person, like Billy Barty, and he was sort of a dwarf when he was young. And then the doctors tried out some new drug that had to do with the pituitary gland and they gave Walter these shots. He grew up to 6 and a half feet tall in about two years. It was too much of a jump. It did something funny to his body, but his voice was always the same. My son, Donovan Freberg, took over the role of Myron in my new *United States* album."

Walter's unfortunate appearance was probably at least part of the reason for his new clown act, with which he entertained children at hospitals and his own shut-in friends. The heavy make-up was ideal to hide behind. When he began the act or of what it consisted is open to speculation. Walter saved some pictures of himself (one of the few things from his later years still found in his scrapbooks), several of which showed a second, female clown. A double act, perhaps?

A few of the promotional photos Walter had made for his clown act.

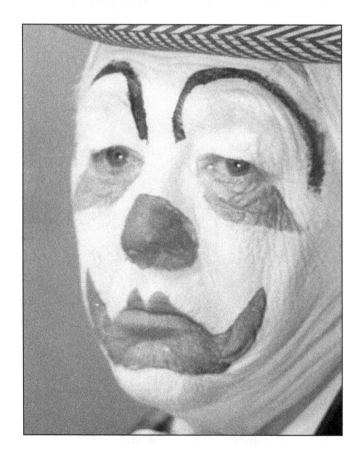

After Walter had been hospitalized for nearly a year, he came out of the accident having to walk with a cane, and later was confined to a wheelchair.

Luckily his physical condition and skin complaints were overcome enough to have secured a few jobs in his last years.

On December 9, 1972 Walter's new Hanna-Barbera cartoon special, *A Christmas Story,* aired. Tetley played Timmy who had written a letter to Santa which had accidentally fallen behind a table. When a kind-hearted mouse called Gumdrop (voiced by Daws Butler) found it, he and Timmy's huge dog Goober (voiced by Paul Winchell) sought out Santa Claus to give him the letter. They escaped the terror of four mischievous cats and finally found Santa descending a chimney. To reach him Gumdrop put the letter in a glider and sailed it towards his sleigh. It sailed too high and went over the roof into the snow. Dejected, the two friends returned home and fell asleep. Later, they were awakened by the joyous shouts of Timmy who was thrilled to find his special request

granted: "Peace on Earth" was written in the sky by the magical glow of Santa's sleigh. As Santa left, he yelled, "Merry Christmas to all, and to all a good night." It was just the sort of wish Walter Tetley himself would have asked for.

The cast of voices was one of the best assembled. Janet Waldo played the mother/girl. Don Messick, the dad and squirrel. Hal Smith was Santa and Fatcat, with John Stephenson as Polecat, Postman and First Dog. The special was written by Ken Spears and Joe Ruby, dotted with songs ("Christmas Story," "Hope," "Where Do You Love?" and "Which One is the Real Santa Claus?") by Denby Williams and Joseph Roland.

The recording was fun, but painful for Walter who continued to complain about the pain in his legs. But he needed to get back on track financially after all the doctor and hospital bills. Most of all, he needed to keep mentally active. Voicing commercials was lucrative, if difficult to obtain. Around 1973 he was heard as a newspaper boy in a Keebler's cookie commercial.

Tetley's last radio work was on a five-part episode of *The Hollywood Radio Theater* entitled "The Princess Stakes Murder." This unique series was narrated by Rod Sterling and was one of the last recorded syndicated series aired over the Mutual Network.

But apart from the odd job, no one knew what had happened to Walter or where he was living. Paul Frees thought he was living in a trailer near the beach.

On June 17, 1975 Walter was admitted to the Beverly Manor Convalescent Hospital at 7940 Topanga Canyon Boulevard in Canoga Park, California. On September 7, 1975 at 12:25 a.m. Walter Campbell Tetley died there. He was 60 years old. The death certificate stated,

"Approximate interval between onset and death – 10 weeks." He gave his last employer as Hanna-Barbera and his last/usual address as 22858 Collins Street in Woodland Hills, Los Angeles. Though he may have been living at the Encino Oaks Motor Lodge free of charge, as it was run by Tetley's friend Jack W. Butts. There was no autopsy, and no family survivors. Walter was cremated on September 10, 1975 at Oakwood Memorial Park, and the remains were buried there. (Though subsequent research shows no record of him under the name of Tetley or Tetzlaff at Oakwood.)

Services were held at 2 p.m. at Reseda Masonic Temple on 6701 Darby Avenue where Walter was an active member. Interment was private.

Jack W. Butts, owner/manager of the Encino Oaks Motor Lodge at 17323 Ventura Blvd. was named executor of Tetley's estate. One of Walter's last wishes was that any monies owed to him by the Screen Actors Guild (he was member #13696 of the Los Angeles branch) for his film work were to go to the Boy Scout troop he helped establish. $2800 was secured from his pension fund and given to the troop.

Epilogue
or, Why This Book Is

CHARLES STUMPF, WHO FOR YEARS compiled information for the definitive book on Fibber McGee and Molly called *Heavenly Days*, had been in touch with the various members of the series. Among the many surviving cast members he interviewed was Hal Peary.

"In November of the year that Walter Tetley died," Stumpf explained, "I was contacted by the executor of Walter's estate, at the suggestion of Hal Peary, asking if I could help compile a list of Tetley's film credits between the years 1938 and 1959, in order that a death benefit could be obtained from the Screen Actor's Guild and donated to one of Walter's favorite charities. I was indeed happy to comply. On April 4, 1976 I was informed that a death benefit had been obtained, and the full amount donated to the Rainbow Scholarship Fund to aid handicapped children.

"At the time I had asked Jack Butts, the executor of the estate, if there might be any old photographs or clippings pertaining to Walter's career, which were to be disposed of. I was sent his personal scrapbooks containing photos and clippings covering his entire career. In addition, I was also sent a small black notebook in which Walter's father had kept a careful accounting of each of his appearances—beginning with the first radio show on February 9, 1930. The book is complete through April 13, 1938—and in that span of time the ambitious actor had chalked up 2,961 appearances—and that was just the beginning of his long career.

"These priceless items are excellent reference material as well as treasured mementos of a most distinguished career. I shall be eternally grateful to Mr. Butts for his kindness."

After Mr. Stumpf's death, whoever inherited his estate did not seem to mind that Tetley's lovely scrapbooks had been pulled apart and sold in pieces on eBay. Luckily I found them and bought them, though it breaks my heart to see them gutted and ripped up like this. At least what remains is safe now.

Writing a book on Tetley 25 years after the scrapbooks had been discovered by Stumpf proved difficult in assembling supplementary material. Jack Butts ran the Encino Oaks Motor Lodge at 17323 Ventura Boulevard, Encino, CA 91316. But writing to the Encino Chamber of Commerce furnished no leads as to Butts or his Motor Lodge. I was told there was no record of the business. Walter more than likely was living at Butts' Lodge in the last years of his life, crippled by hospital debts and a lack of work. Unfortunately, without a witness, it's difficult to guess about Walter's last years.

The Encino Chamber of Commerce likewise had no information on The Happy Tail, his pet shop. Neither could the Boy Scouts help with the troop that Walter founded or led for who knows how many years. No one who responded knew anything about Boy Scout Troop 1260 or the gift of money that Walter left them.

The quest for information beyond what was contained in the scrapbooks was mostly dead ends. There are no known family survivors. Though there are still some people out there that Walter worked with, no one *knew* him. They all had good, general things to say about the man who kept his small boy's voice, but could furnish no specific leads.

Stan Freberg didn't return my calls or letters, but luckily Larry Gassman gave me a copy of the lengthy interview he and his brother did with Stan when he was promoting his *USA Vol. 2* album. June Foray is a lovely person, but unfortunately she was one of many who did not get to know Walter. Don Pitts, Walter's last agent, was helpful with a few good stories; he was certainly the best "witness" I could find for the first edition. For the second edition, there is delightful *new* information from his cousin Angus Campbell and WWII buddy Ira Cochin. But it's still not enough.

You would think that with all the leads I had—social security number, SAG number, address, etc., etc.—that I could come up with some significant additional material. But no. And that's why I again urge anyone reading this book—especially a good friend with some stories to tell—to get in touch. I'd love to put out a *third* edition that will fill in some of the holes in this book. Otherwise, it will have to live as it stands.

Speaking of SAG, I faxed them Walter's information and SAG number (13696), but was told, "If Mr. Tetley did not do any work on an S.A.G.-signatory film that commenced AFTER January 31, 1960, there will be no residuals to his estate." Since Walter's only recurring work after 1960 seemed to be the Jay Ward series, and since SAG did not have to keep his estate information on file, obviously nothing was or is being paid into that estate. Had there been, it probably would have gone to the Boy Scouts troop (if it still existed after Walter's demise) or to Jack Butts, another probably deceased witness to the Tetley legend.

Walter Tetley may remain a mystery of history, but Leroy, Julius, Sherman and all the rest of his characters will forever live on to delight new generations. Comic genius will be recognized.

– Ben Ohmart
April 2016

Credits

RADIO SHOWS

Listed in the little black notebook

[Titles in ( ) have no show number listed, therefore they are public appearances or auditions. Though the notebook lists what show number this was for Walter, as they are all consecutive I have left these numbers out. When a number appears in ( ) after a show title, it usually denotes a repeat broadcast for the west coast. Walter's first radio show was the February 9, 1930 *Children's Hour*. The first page is missing in this notebook, but all shows are consecutive starting on July 13, which was Walter's 49th show.

The credits have been kept as they were originally written in the notebook, with author notes in [ ] for the sake of clarity. P.A. = personal appearance.

1930

February 9 – Children's Hour
February 15 – Barn Show [With Madge Tucker]
February 16 – Children's Hour
February 22 – Barn Show
February 23 – Children's Hour
July 13 – Children's Hour
July 17 – Lady Next Door
July 19 – Lady Next Door
July 20 – Children's Hour
July 23 – Lady Next Door
July 26 – Lady Next Door
July 27 – Children's Hour
August 1 – Lady Next Door
August 2 – Lady Next Door
August 3 – Children's Hour
August 7 – Lady Next Door
August 9 – Lady Next Door
August 10 – Children's Hour
August 11 – Lady Next Door
August 17 – Children's Hour
August 20 – Lady Next Door
August 23 – Lady Next Door

August 24 – Children's Hour
August 27 – Lady Next Door
August 28 – Lady Next Door
August 31 – Children's Hour
September 1 – Lady Next Door
September 3 – Lady Next Door
September 6 – Lady Next Door
September 7 – Children's Hour
September 12 – Lady Next Door
September 13 – Lady Next Door
September 14 – Children's Hour
September 15 – Lady Next Door
September 17 – Lady Next Door
September 20 – Lady Next Door
September 21 – Children's Hour
September 24 – Lady Next Door
September 25 – Lady Next Door
September 27 – Lady Next Door
September 28 – Children's Hour
September 30 – Lady Next Door
October 1 – Lady Next Door
October 4 – Lady Next Door
October 4 – Dixie Circus
October 5 – Children's Hour
October 8 – Lady Next Door

October 10 – Lady Next Door
October 12 – Children's Hour
October 13 – Lady Next Door
October 18 – Lady Next Door
October 19 – Children's Hour
October 22 – Lady Next Door
October 23 – Lady Next Door
October 24 – Lady Next Door
October 25 – Lady Next Door
October 26 – Children's Hour
October 29 – Lady Next Door
October 30 – Lady Next Door
October 31 – Lady Next Door
November 1 – Lady Next Door
November 2 – Children's Hour
November 3 – Lady Next Door
November 5 – Lady Next Door
November 6 – Lady Next Door
November 8 – Household
November 8 – Lady Next Door
November 9 – Children's Hour
November 13 – Lady Next Door
November 15 – Lady Next Door
November 16 – Children's Hour
November 19 – Lady Next Door
November 20 – Lady Next Door
November 21 – Lady Next Door
November 22 – Lady Next Door
November 23 – Children's Hour
November 26 – Lady Next Door
November 28 – Lady Next Door
November 28 – Mason J.C. [P.A. –
    People's Palace, Jersey City, NJ]
November 30 – Children's Hour
December 1 – Lady Next Door
December 3 – Lady Next Door
December 5 – Lady Next Door
December 5 – Yonkers [P.A.]
December 7 – Children's Hour
December 8 – Lady Next Door
December 9 – Lady Next Door
December 10 – Lady Next Door
December 13 – Lady Next Door
December 14 – Children's Hour
December 15 – Lady Next Door
December 17 – Lady Next Door
December 18 – Lady Next Door
December 20 – Lady Next Door
December 21 – Children's Hour
December 22 – Lady Next Door

December 23 – Lady Next Door
December 24 – Lady Next Door
December 25 – Lady Next Door
December 27 – Lady Next Door
December 28 – Children's Hour
December 29 – Lady Next Door
December 30 – Lady Next Door

1931

January 3 – Lady Next Door
January 4 – Children's Hour
January 5 – Lady Next door
January 7 – Lady Next Door
January 8 – Lady Next Door
January 10 – Lady Next Door
January 10 – Eastern Star [National
    Women's Organization. Installation
    dinner at Pythian – Temple, New
    York City]
January 11 – Children's Hour
January 12 – Lady Next Door
January 15 – Lady Next Door
January 17 – Lady Next Door
January 18 – Children's Hour
January 19 – Lady Next Door
January 23 – Lady Next Door
January 24 – Lady Next Door
January 25 – Children's Hour
January 26 – Lady Next Door
January 29 – Lady Next Door
January 31 – Lady Next Door
February 1 – Children's Hour
February 2 – Lady Next Door
February 4 – Lady Next Door
February 5 – Lady Next Door
February 5 – Raising Jr.
February 6 – Raising Jr.
February 7 – Lady Next Door
February 7 – Dixie Circus
February 7 – Ku Ku Hour [The Cukoo
    Hour]
February 8 – Children's Hour
February 9 – Lady Next Door
February 11 – Raising Jr.
February 12 – Lady Next Door
February 14 – Lady Next Door
February 15 – Children's Hour
February 16 – Lady Next Door

February 19 – Lady Next Door
February 19 – Raising Jr.
February 21 – Scranton, PA [P.A. Jr.
    O.U.A. Country Club]
February 22 – Children's Hour
February 23 – Maltine
February 24 – Lady Next Door
February 26 – Lady Next door
February 26 – Niaraga Hudson
February 27 – Raising Jr.
February 27 – Uncle Abe & David
February 28 – Lady Next Door
March 1 – Children's Hour
March 2 – Lady Next Door
March 4 – Lady Next Door
March 4 – Raising Jr.
March 5 – Lady Next Door
March 5 – Rapid Transit [These are
    possibly live radio commercials]
March 6 – Lady Next Door
March 7 – Lady Next Door
March 8 – Children's Hour
March 8 – Raising Jr.
March 9 – Lady Next Door
March 10 – Rapid Transit
March 11 – Lady Next Door
March 11 – (Yonkers)
March 12 – Lady Next Door
March 13 – Lady Next Door
March 14 – Lady Next Door
March 14 – (Eastern Star M.C.)
March 15 – Children's Hour
March 16 – Lady Next Door
March 18 – Lady Next Door
March 19 – Lady Next Door
March 21 – Lady Next Door
March 22 – Children's Hour
March 23 – Lady Next Door
March 25 – Lady Next Door
March 26 – Lady Next Door
March 26 – Rapid Transit
March 28 – Lady Next Door
March 29 – Children's Hour
March 30 – Lady Next Door
March 30 – Raising Jr.
March 31 – Rapid Transit
April 1 – Lady Next Door
April 2 – Lady Next Door
April 2 – Rapid Transit
April 4 – Lady Next Door

April 5 – Children's Hour
April 6 – Lady Next Door
April 7 – (Rockville Center) [Benefit for
    South Nassau Community Hospital
    in New – York]
April 8 – Lady Next Door
April 9 – Lady Next Door
April 9 – Rapid Transit
April 11 – Lady Next Door
April 11 – (Eastern Star M.C.)
April 12 – Children's Hour
April 13 – Lady Next Door
April 15 – Lady Next Door
April 16 – Lady Next Door
April 18 – Lady Next Door
April 18 – Ku Ku Hour
April 19 – Children's Hour
April 19 – Colliers Hour
April 20 – Lady Next Door
April 22 – Lady Next Door
April 23 – Lady Next Door
April 25 – Lady Next Door
April 26 – Children's Hour
April 27 – Lady Next Door
April 28 – Raising Jr.
April 29 – Lady Next Door
April 30 – Lady Next Door
May 1 – (Pottstown, PA) [At the Victor
    Theater]
May 2 – Lady Next Door
May 2 – (Union City Mason)
May 3 – Children's Hour
May 4 – Lady Next Door
May 6 – (Morris Plan, NJ)
May 7 – Lady Next Door
May 8 – (Audition)
May 9 – Lady Next Door
May 10 – Children's Hour
May 10 – Mother's Days [Probably
    special "Mother's Day" broadcast]
May 10 – National Dairy
May 11 – Lady Next Door
May 11 – (Audition)
May 13 – Lady Next Door
May 13 – Raising Jr.
May 14 – Lady Next Door
May 16 – Lady Next Door
May 17 – Children's Hour
May 18 – Lady Next Door
May 20 – Lady Next Door

May 21 – Lady Next Door
May 22 – Lady Next Door
May 22 – Raising Jr.
May 23 – Lady Next Door
May 23 – (St. Mitz. Nurses)
May 24 – Children's Hour
May 25 – Eno [The Eno Crime Club]
May 25 – Lady Next Door
May 26 – Eno
May 27 – Lady Next Door
May 27 – Eno
May 28 – Lady Next Door
May 28 – Eno
May 29 – Eno
May 30 – Lady Next Door
May 30 – Eno
May 31 – Children's Hour
June 1 – Lux [Lux Radio Theater]
June 3 – Lady Next Door
June 4 – Lady Next Door
June 5 – Lady Next Door
June 6 – Lady Next Door
June 7 – Children's Hour
June 8 – Lady Next Door
June 9 – Raising Jr.
June 10 – Lady Next Door
June 12 – Raising Jr.
June 13 – Lady Next Door
June 14 – Children's Hour
June 14 – Emerald Isle
June 15 – Lady Next Door
June 17 – (Audition)
June 18 – Lady Next Door
June 20 – Lady Next Door
June 21 – Children's Hour
June 22 – Lady Next Door
June 23 – Raising Jr.
June 23 – (Audition)
June 24 – Lady Next Door
June 25 – Lady Next Door
June 26 – Lady Next Door
June 27-30 – (Franklin Theatre)
July 2 – Lady Next Door
July 3 – Lady Next Door
July 3 – Raising Jr.
July 4 – (Bayville)
July 5 – Children's Hour
July 5 – Emerald Isle
July 5 – (Trenton, NJ)
July 8 – Lady Next Door

July 9 – Lady Next Door
July 9 – Niaraga Hudson [P.A.]
July 11 – Lady Next Door
July 12 – Children's Hour
July 12 – Emerald Isle
July 12 – (Mrs. Seeley Flusing) [P.A. Flushing, NY]
July 13 – Lady Next Door
July 15 – Lady Next Door
July 16 – Allentown, PA [P.A. Picnic for St. Paul's Lutheran Sunday school]
July 17 – Raising Jr.
July 18 – Lady Next Door
July 19 – Children's Hour
July 20 – Lady Next Door
July 22-24 – (86 St. Theatre)
July 25 – (Adamstown, PA)
July 26 – Children's Hour
July 27 – Lady Next Door
July 28 – Raising Jr.
July 29 – Lady Next Door
July 30 – Lady Next Door
August 1 – Lady Next Door
August 2 – Children's Hour
August 2 – Emerald Isle
August 2 – (Trenton, NJ)
August 3 – (Audition)
August 5 – Lady Next Door
August 6 – Lady Next Door
August 8 – Lady Next Door
August 9 – Children's Hour
August 9 – Emerald Isle
August 10 – Lady Next Door
August 11 – Raising Jr.
August 12-13 – (Claramont, NY)
August 15 – (Adamstown, PA)
August 16 – Children's Hour
August 17 – Lady Next Door
August 18 – Lady Next Door
August 20 – Lady Next Door
August 21 – Lady Next Door
August 22 – Lady Next Door
August 23 – Children's Hour
August 24 – Lady Next Door
August 26 – Lady Next Door
August 26 – (Audition)
August 27 – Lady Next Door
August 27 – (Audition)
August 28 – Lady Next Door
August 29 – Constitution Trip

August 30 – Emerald Isle
August 31 – Lady Next Door
September 1 – Lady Next Door
September 1 – (Flushing Rotary)
September 2 – Lady Next Door
September 3 – Lady Next Door
September 3 – (Audition)
September 6 – Children's Hour
September 6 – Emerald Isle
September 7 – True Story
September 8 – Lady Next Door
September 9 – Lady Next Door
September 9 – Women's Radio Rev.
September 10 – Lady Next Door
September 11 – Lady Next Door
September 12 – Lady Next Door
September 13 – Children's Hour
September 13 – Emerald Isle
September 14 – Lady Next Door
September 15 – Lady Next Door
September 15 – (Audition)
September 15 – Raising Jr.
September 16 – Household [Big Time
     Radio Household]
September 16 – (Asbury Park)
September 17 – (Audition)
September 19 – Lady Next Door
September 20 – Children's Hour
September 23 – Lady Next Door
September 24 – Lady Next Door
September 25 – (Washington D.C.)
September 26 – Lady Next Door
September 27 – Children's Hour
September 27 – Emerald Isle
September 28 – Lady Next Door
September 30 – Lady Next Door
October 1 – Lady Next Door
October 4 – Children's Hour
October 5 – True Story
October 6 – Maltine
October 7 – Bordens
October 7 – Lady Next Door
October 8 – Lady Next Door
October 8 – Raising Jr.
October 11 – Children's Hour
October 11 – Emerald Isle
October 12 – Lady Next Door
October 13 – Maltine
October 14 – Lady Next Door
October 15 – Lady Next Door

October 17 – Lady Next Door
October 18 – Children's Hour
October 18 – Emerald Isle
October 19 – Lady Next Door
October 20 – Lady Next Door
October 21 – Lady Next Door
October 22 – Lady Next Door
October 25 – Children's Hour
October 25 – Emerald Isle
October 26 – Lady Next Door
October 28 – Lady Next Door
October 29 – Lady Next Door
October 30 – Lady Next Door
October 30 – General Electric
October 31 – Lady Next Door
November 1 – Children's Hour
November 1 – Emerald Isle
November 3 – Lady Next Door
November 3 – Raising Jr.
November 5 – Lady Next Door
November 6 – Lady Next Door
November 6 – General Electric
November 7 – Lady Next Door
November 8 – Children's Hour
November 8 – Emerald Isle
November 9 – Lady Next Door
November 10 – Raising Jr.
November 11 – Household
November 12 – Lady Next Door
November 13 – Lady Next Door
November 14 – (Eastern Star)
November 15 – Children's Hour
November 15 – Emerald Isle
November 16 – Lady Next Door
November 16 – True Story
November 18 – Lady Next Door
November 19 – Lady Next Door
November 20 – Lady Next Door
November 20 – March of Time
November 21 – Lady Next Door
November 22 – Children's Hour
November 22 – Emerald Isle
November 22 – Raising Jr.
November 23 – Lady Next Door
November 23 – True Story
November 25 – Lady Next Door
November 27 – Lady Next Door
November 27 – Raising Jr.
November 28 – Lady Next Door
November 29 – Children's Hour

November 29 – Emerald Isle
November 30 – Lady Next Door
November 30 – Raising Jr.
December 2 – Lady Next Door
December 3 – Lady Next Door
December 4 – Raising Jr.
December 5 – Lady Next Door
December 6 – Children's Hour
December 6 – Emerald Isle
December 7 – Lady Next Door
December 7 – Raising Jr.
December 8 – Maltine
December 9 – (Hightstown, N.J.)
December 13 – Raising Jr.
December 14 – Lady Next Door
December 16 – Lady Next Door

December 18 – Lady Next Door
December 19 – Lady Next Door
December 19 – Raising Jr.
December 20 – Children's Hour
December 20 – Emerald Isle
December 21 – Lady Next Door
December 22 – Maltine
December 23 – Lady Next Door
December 24 – Lady Next Door
December 25 – Lady Next Door
December 25 – Lady Next Door C.P.
    (Command Performance?)
December 27 – Children's Hour
December 27 – Emerald Isle
December 27 – Raising Jr.
December 28 – Lady Next Door

December 28 – Raising Jr.
December 29 – Lady Next Door
December 30 – Lady Next Door
December 31 – Children's Hour

1932

January 1 – Raising Jr.
January 2 – Lady Next Door
January 3 – Children's Hour
January 3 – Emerald Isle
January 3 – Raising Jr.
January 4 – Lady Next Door
January 5 – Maltine
January 6 – Lady Next Door
January 9 – Raising Jr.
January 10 – Children's Hour
January 10 – Emerald Isle
January 11 – Lady Next Door
January 12 – Maltine
January 13 – Lady Next Door
January 14 – Lady Next Door
January 14 – Raising Jr.
January 16 – Lady Next Door
January 17 – Children's Hour
January 17 – Emerald Isle
January 18 – Lady Next Door
January 20 – Lady Next Door
January 22 – Lady Next Door
January 22 – Raising Jr.
January 24 – Children's Hour
January 24 – Emerald Isle
January 25 – Lady Next Door
January 26 – Lady Next Door
January 27 – Lady Next Door
January 28 – Lady Next Door
January 29 – Raising Jr.
January 30 – Household
January 30 – Lady Next Door
January 31 – Children's Hour
January 31 – Emerald Isle
February 1 – Lady Next Door
February 1 – Raising Jr.
February 3 – Lady Next Door
February 4 – Lady Next Door
February 7 – Lady Next Door
February 7 – Children's Hour
February 9 – Raising Jr.
February 10 – Lady Next Door
February 12 – Lady Next Door
February 13 – Raising Jr.
February 14 – Children's Hour
February 15 – Lady Next Door
February 17 – Lady Next Door
February 18 – Lady Next Door
February 19 – Raising Jr.
February 20 – Lady Next Door
February 21 – Children's Hour
February 21 – Emerald Isle
February 21 – Raising Jr.
February 22 – Raising Jr.
February 23 – Lady Next Door
February 25 – Lady Next Door
February 26 – Lady Next Door
February 28 – Children's Hour
February 28 – Emerald Isle
February 29 – Lady Next Door
March 2 – Lady Next Door
March 4 – Friendship Town
March 5 – Lady Next Door
March 5 – Raising Jr.
March 6 – Children's Hour
March 7 – Lady Next Door
March 9 – Lady Next Door
March 10 – Lady Next Door
March 10 – Raising Jr.
March 11 – Lady Next Door
March 12 – Lady Next Door
March 13 – Children's Hour
March 14 – Lady Next Door
March 16 – Lady Next Door
March 17 – Lady Next Door
March 20 – Children's Hour
March 21 – Lady Next Door
March 21 – Raising Jr.
March 23 – Lady Next Door
March 24 – Lady Next Door
March 26 – Lady Next Door
March 27 – Children's Hour
March 28 – Lady Next Door
March 30 – Lady Next Door
April 1 – Friendship Town
April 2 – Lady Next Door
April 3 – Children's Hour
April 4 – Lady Next Door
April 5 – Household
April 5 – (Hackensack, NJ)
April 6 – Lady Next Door
April 9 – Lady Next Door

April 9 – Raising Jr.
April 10 – Children's Hour
April 11 – Children's Hour
April 13 – Lady Next Door
April 14 – Lady Next Door
April 15 – (Coaldale, PA)
April 17 – Children's Hour
April 17 – Raising Jr.
April 18 – Lady Next Door
April 18 – Household
April 19 – Lady Next Door
April 21 – Lady Next Door
April 22 – (Kingstown, PA) [P.A. Band
    concert in high school auditorium]
April 23 – Lady Next Door
April 24 – Children's Hour
April 25 – Lady Next Door
April 26 – (Bogato, NJ)
April 27 – Lady Next Door
April 25 (or 28) – Household
April 28 – Du Pont
April 29 – Household
April 30 – Lady Next Door
April 30 – Hap Tulliver
May 1 – Children's Hour
May 2 – Lady Next Door
May 4 – Lady Next Door
May 6 – Friendship Town
May 7 – Lady Next Door
May 7 – Hap Tulliver
May 8 – Children's Hour
May 9 – Lady Next Door
May 11 – Lady Next Door
May 12 – Lady Next Door
May 14 – (Lowlow, MA) [Ludlow, MA]
May 15 – Children's Hour
May 16 – Household
May 18 – Lady Next Door
May 19 – Lady Next Door
May 21 – Lady Next Door
May 22 – Children's Hour
May 23 – Household
May 23 – Lady Next Door
May 25 – Lady Next Door
May 26 – Lady Next Door
May 28 – Lady Next Door
May 29 – Children's Hour
May 30 – Lady Next Door
June 1 – Lady Next Door
June 2 – Lady Next Door

June 4 – Lady Next Door
June 5 – Children's Hour
June 6 – Household
June 6 – Lady Next Door
June 6 – Tasty Yeast
June 7 – Lady Next Door
June 8 – Mother's Day
June 8 – Lady Next Door
June 10 – Friendship Town
June 12 – Children's Hour
June 13 – Household
June 13 – Lady Next Door
June 13 – Tasty Yeast
June 15 – Big Time
June 15 – Lady Next Door
June 17 – Friendship Town
June 18 – Lady Next Door
June 19 – Children's Hour
June 19 – Father's Day
June 20 – Lady Next Door
June 20 – (audition)
June 22 – Lady Next Door
June 23 – Lady Next Door
June 24 – Lady Next Door
June 25 – Lady Next Door
June 26 – Children's Hour
June 27 – Lady Next Door
June 27 – Tasty Yeast
June 28 – ?
June 28 – Joe Palooka
June 29 – Lady Next Door
June 30 – Lady Next Door
July 1 – Lady Next Door
July 2 – (audition)
July 3 – Children's Hour
July 4 – Household
July 5 – Lady Next Door
July 6 – Lady Next Door
July 8 – Lady Next Door
July 8 – (audition)
July 9 – Lady Next Door
July 9 – East Lynn
July 10 – Children's Hour
July 11 – Household
July 11 – Lady Next Door
July 12 – Lady Next Door
July 13 – Lady Next Door
July 14 – Lady Next Door
July 15 – Lady Next Door
July 16 – Lady Next Door

July 17 – Children's Hour
July 18 – Household
July 18 – Lady Next Door
July 19 – Lady Next Door
July 20 – Lady Next Door
July 21 – Lady Next Door
July 22 – (Claremont, NY)
July 24 – Children's Hour
July 25 – Household
July 26 – Skyscraper
July 27 – Lady Next Door
July 28 – Lady Next Door
July 29 – Lady Next Door
July 30 – Lady Next Door
July 31 – Children's Hour
August 1 – Lady Next Door
August 2 – Lady Next Door
August 3 – Lady Next Door
August 4 – (New Rochelle) [P.A. in New
    York]
August 5 – Lady Next Door
August 6 – Lady Next Door
August 7 – Children's Hour
August 7 – Silver Flute
August 8 – Lady Next Door
August 8 – Household
August 9 – Lady Next Door
August 10 – (audition)
August 12 – Lady Next Door
August 13 – Lady Next Door
August 14 – Children's Hour
August 15 – Household
August 15 – Lady Next Door
August 16 – Lady Next Door
August 18 – Lady Next Door
August 22 – Household
August 22 – Lady Next Door
August 23 – Lady Next Door
August 25 – Lady Next Door
August 26 – Lady Next Door
August 27 – Lady Next Door
August 28 – Children's Hour
August 28 – Chase & Sanborn
August 29 – Household
August 29 – Lady Next Door
August 31 – Lady Next Door
September 4 – Children's Hour
September 4 – Household
September 5 – Lady Next Door
September 6 – Lady Next Door

September 8 – Lady Next Door
September 9 – Lady Next Door
September 11 – Children's Hour
September 12 – Household
September 13 – Lady Next Door
September 14 – Lady Next Door
September 15 – Lady Next Door
September 16 – Lady Next Door
September 16 – (mike test)
September 18 – Children's Hour
September 20 – Friendship Town
September 21 – Lady Next Door
September 22 – Lady Next Door
September 23 – Lady Next Door
September 24 – Lady Next Door
September 25 – Children's Hour
September 26 – Revolving Stage
September 26 – Lady Next Door
September 27 – Lady Next Door
September 28 – Lady Next Door
September 29 – Lady Next Door
September 30 – Lady Next Door
October 2 – Children's Hour
October 3 – Lady Next Door
October 5 – Lady Next Door
October 6 – Household
October 6 – Lady Next Door
October 8 – Littmann's [Possibly
    commercial for the large
    department store]
October 9 – Children's Hour
October 10 – Lady Next Door
October 11 – Wheatenaville
October 12 – Flying Family
October 13 – Household
October 13 – Lady Next Door
October 14 – Littmann's
October 14 – Wayside Cottage
October 14 – Lady Next Door
October 15 – Lady Next Door
October 16 – Children's Hour
October 17 – Lady Next Door
October 17 – (audition)
October 17 – (audition)
October 18 – Lady Next Door
October 19 – Lady Next Door
October 20 – Lady Next Door
October 20 – Household
October 21 – Records [Recording
    transcribed shows]

A 1936 publicity photo.

October 22 – Littmann's
October 22 – (audition)
October 22 – Records
October 23 – Children's Hour
October 24 – Lady Next Door
October 24 – (audition)
October 25 – Lady Next Door
October 26 – Lady Next Door
October 27 – Records
October 27 – Household
October 29 – Lady Next Door
October 30 – Children's Hour
October 31 – Wayside Cottage
October 31 – (audition)

November 1 – Records
November 2 – Flying Family
November 2 – Lady Next Door
November 3 – Household
November 3 – Country Doctor
November 4 – Lady Next Door
November 4 – Unemployed [Possibly a
    commercial for the Unemployment
    Office]
November 5 – Littmann's
November 5 – Lady Next Door
November 6 – Children's Hour
November 7 – Lady Next Door
November 8 – Lady Next Door

November 9 – Lady Next Door
November 10 – Household
November 10 – Death Valley Days
November 11 – Lady Next Door
November 11 – March of Time
November 12 – Prospect Theatre
November 13 – Prospect Theatre
November 14 – Prospect Theatre
November 15 – Prospect Theatre
November 16 – Lady Next Door
November 16 – Wheatenaville
November 17 – Lady Next Door
November 17 – (Eastern Star E.W.)
November 18 – (audition)
November 18 – Lady Next Door
November 18 – (Yonkers P.T.A.)
November 19 – Littmann's
November 20 – Children's Hour
November 21 – Records (two)
November 22 – Lady Next Door
November 23 – Records (three)
November 24 – Death Valley Days
November 25 – Lady Next Door
November 25 – March of Time
November 26 – Littmann's
November 26 – Lady Next Door
November 27 – Children's Hour
November 27 – Red Adams
November 28 – Wheatenaville
November 29 – (audition)
November 29 – (bazaar)
November 30 – (Pathe)
November 30 – Records
December 1 – Lady Next Door
December 2 – Lady Next Door
December 2 – March of Time
December 2 – (audition)
December 2 – (pipe band)
December 3 – Littmann's
December 3 – Lady Next Door
December 4 – Children's Hour
December 4 – Red Adams
December 5 – (audition)
December 7 – Lady Next Door
December 7 – (audition)
December 7 – (audition)
December 7 – (audition)
December 8 – Lady Next Door
December 8 – (audition)
December 8 – (audition)

December 9 – Lady Next Door
December 9 – (Newark Church)
December 10 – Littmann's
December 10 – Lady Next Door
December 11 – Children's Hour
December 12 – Hitting the Keys
    [Probably a local radio show]
December 12 – Records
December 13 – (audition)
December 14 – Hitting the Keys
December 15 – (audition)
December 16 – Hitting the Keys
December 16 – Records (2)
December 16 – Unemployed
December 17 – Littmann's
December 18 – Children's Hour
December 21 – Lady Next Door
December 22 – Lady Next Door
December 23 – Lady Next Door
December 24 – Littmann's
December 24 – Lady Next Door
December 24 – Scrooge [Probably A
    Christmas Carol broadcast]
December 25 – Children's Hour
December 26 – Wheatenaville
December 27-30 – (Bayville Theatre)
December 28 – Five Star
December 28 – Lady Next Door
December 29 – Household
December 29 – (audition)
December 30 – Lady Next Door
December 30 – Records
December 30 – Littmann's

1933

January 1 – Children's Hour
January 3 – (audition)
January 4 – Records
January 5 – Wheatenaville
January 6 – Lady Next Door
January 7 – Lady Next Door
January 8 – Children's Hour
January 9 – Lady Next Door
January 11 – Lady Next Door
January 11 – Wayside Cottage
January 13 – Lady Next Door
January 13 – March of Time
January 14 – Lady Next Door

January 15 – Children's Hour
January 16 – Lady Next Door
January 17 – Wheatenaville
January 17 – Lucky Strike
January 18 – Lady Next Door
January 18 – Wheatenaville
January 18 – (audition)
January 19 – Lady Next Door
January 19 – Wheatenaville
January 20 – Lady Next Door
January 21 – Helen & Mary [The
    Adventures of Helen & Mary]
January 22 – Children's Hour
January 23 – Lady Next Door
January 23 – (audition)
January 24 – (audition)
January 24 – (audition)
January 25 – Lady Next Door
January 25 – (audition)
January 26 – Lady Next Door
January 26 – (audition)
January 27 – (audition)
January 28 – Lady Next Door
January 29 – Children's Hour
January 30 – Lady Next Door
February 1 – Lady Next Door
February 4 – Helen & Mary
February 4 – Lady Next Door
February 5 – Children's Hour
February 6 – Lady Next Door
February 7 – (audition)
February 7 – Wheatenaville
February 8 – Lady Next Door
February 9 – (audition)
February 10 – Lady Next Door
February 10 – (Katonah Fire Company)
    [P.A. in New York]
February 11 – (Pathe)
February 12-20 (audition Socony.)
February 12 – Children's Hour
February 13 – Lincoln Prairie
February 15 – Lady Next Door
February 16 – The Great Jeasper
February 17 – Lady Next Door
February 17 – (audition)
February 19 – Children's Hour
February 20 – Lady Next Door
February 21 – Wheatenaville
February 23 – Lady Next Door
February 23 – Wheatenaville

February 24 – (audition)
February 25 – Helen & Mary
February 25 – Lady Next Door
February 26 – Children's Hour
February 26 – Sloan's
February 27 – Lady Next Door
February 27 – Wheatenaville
March 1 – Lady Next Door
March 2 – Wheatenaville
March 3 – Lady Next Door
March 3 – March of Time
March 4 – Lady Next Door
March 4 – (pictures) [Probably publicity
    photo session]
March 5 – Children's Hour
March 6 – Records
March 6 – Lady Next Door
March 7 – Lady Next Door
March 8 – Buck Rogers
March 9 – Buck Rogers
March 10 – Socony Vac.
March 12 – Children's Hour
March 14 – Lady Next Door
March 16 – Lady Next Door
March 18 – Lady Next Door
March 19 – Children's Hour
March 19 – (Mrs. Seeley)
March 19 – Big Ben
March 20 – Lady Next Door
March 21 – Lady Next Door
March 21 – (audition)
March 22 – Household
March 25 – Lady Next Door
March 26 – Children's Hour
March 26 – Sloan's
March 27 – Lady Next Door
March 28 – Lady Next Door
March 30 – Lady Next Door
March 31 – Records
March 31 – Lady Next Door
April 1 – Helen & Mary
April 1 – Lady Next Door
April 2 – Children's Hour
April 3 – Lady Next Door
April 3 – (audition)
April 3 – Household
April 4 – Lady Next Door
April 5 – Lady Next Door
April 8 – Helen & Mary
April 8 – Lady Next Door

April 8 – Neighbors
April 9 – Children's Hour
April 10 – Lady Next Door
April 11 – Listerine
April 12 – American School of the Air
April 12 – Listerine
April 13 – Records
April 13 – Jack and the Beanstalk
April 14 – Jack and the Beanstalk
April 15 – Lady Next Door
April 15 – Neighbors
April 16 – Children's Hour
April 17 – Lady Next Door
April 17 – Blind Asylum [Probably a P.A. benefit]
April 18 – Lady Next Door
April 18 – Raising Jr.
April 19 – (Jewish home) [Benefit]
April 20 – Lady Next Door
April 22 – Lady Next Door
April 22 – Helen & Mary
April 22 – (audition)
April 22 – Black Beauty
April 23 – Children's Hour
April 24 – (audition)
April 25 – Lady Next Door
April 26 – (audition)
April 27 – Morse Code
April 28 – Bayside Orphan Asylum [Benefit]
April 29 – Helen & Mary
April 29 – Lady Next Door
April 30 – Children's Hour
May 2 – Lady Next Door
May 5 – Socony Vac. [Socony-Vacuum Corporation program AKA Seconyland]
May 6 – Lady Next Door
May 7 – Children's Hour
May 8 – (audition)
May 8 – (audition)
May 9 – Lady Next Door
May 10 – (audition)
May 11 – Lady Next Door
May 13 – Lady Next Door
May 14 – Children's Hour
May 18 – Lady Next Door
May 19 – (audition)
May 20 – Lady Next Door
May 20 – Square Club

May 21 – Children's Hour
May 22 – (audition)
May 22 – (audition)
May 23 – Lady Next Door
May 23 – (audition)
May 23 – (audition)
May 25 – Lady Next Door
May 27 – Lady Next Door
May 27 – (Ned Wayburn)
May 28 – Children's Hour
May 29 – Lady Next Door
May 30 – Lady Next Door
June 2 – Socony Vac.
June 2 – (audition)
June 3 – Lady Next Door
June 4 – Children's Hour
June 5 – (audition)
June 6 – Lady Next Door
June 6 – (audition)
June 7 – (audition)
June 8 – (audition)
June 8 – Lady Next Door
June 9 – (audition)
June 10 – Helen & Mary
June 10 – Lady Next Door
June 11 – Children's Hour
June 12 – (audition)
June 13 – (audition)
June 17 – Lady Next Door
June 17 – (Ned Wayburn)
June 18 – Children's Hour
June 19 – Radio Guild
June 21 – (audition)
June 21 – Winnie the Pooh
June 23 – Winnie the Pooh
June 23 – Robinson
June 24 – Lady Next Door
June 25 – Children's Hour
June 25 – Page of Romance
June 26 – Lady Next Door
June 26 – (audition)
June 27 – Lady Next Door
June 28 – Lady Next Door
June 29 – Lady Next Door
June 29 – (audition)
July 1 – Lady Next Door
July 1 – Helen & Mary
July 2 – Children's Hour
July 3 – Lady Next Door
July 5 – Winnie the Pooh

July 8 – Helen & Mary
July 8 – Lady Next Door
July 9 – Children's Hour
July 10 – Drake's Drums
July 10 – Soconyland
July 11 – Lady Next Door
July 11 – Rex Cole
July 12 – Lady Next Door
July 12 – Winnie the Pooh
July 12 – Stephen Foster
July 14 – Winnie the Pooh
July 15 – Lady Next Door
July 17 – (audition)
July 17 – (audition)
July 17 – Drake's Drums
July 18 – (audition)
July 18 – Lady Next Door
July 19 – Winnie the Pooh
July 19 – Stephen Foster
July 20 – Lady Next Door
July 20 – (Pathe)
July 21 – (test)
July 22 – Lady Next Door
July 22 – (audition)
July 23 – Children's Hour
July 24 – Records
July 25 – Lady Next Door
July 25 – (audition)
July 26 – Lady Next Door
July 26 – (audition)
July 27 – Lady Next Door
July 29 – Lady Next Door
August 1 – Lady Next Door
August 2 – (audition)
August 3 – Lady Next Door
August 4 – (audition)
August 6 – Children's Hour
August 7 – (audition)
August 7 – (audition)
August 7 – (audition)
August 7 – Lady Next Door
August 8 – Lady Next Door
August 8 – (audition)
August 8 – (audition)
August 9 – (audition)
August 9 – (audition)
August 9 – (audition)
August 12 – Lady Next Door
August 13 – Children's Hour
August 14 – Lady Next Door

August 15 – Lady Next Door
August 16 – (audition)
August 17 – Lady Next Door
August 19 – Lady Next Door
August 20 – Children's Hour
August 21 – Drake's Drums
August 22 – (audition)
August 23 – Lady Next Door
August 23 – (audition)
August 23 – (audition)
August 24 – Show Boat
August 27 – Children's Hour
August 28 – Lady Next Door
August 28 – Drake's Drums
August 29 – Lady Next Door
August 30 – Lady Next Door
August 31 – Lady Next Door
August 31 – (audition)
September 2 – The Sun
September 3 – Children's Hour
September 5 – Lady Next Door
September 5 – (audition)
September 5 – Rex Cole
September 6 – Lady Next Door
September 7 – Krakts
September 8 – Hellmann's
September 9 – Lady Next Door
September 10 – Children's Hour
September 12 – Lady Next Door
September 12 – Eno
September 13 – Eno
September 13 – (audition)
September 14 – (audition)
September 16 – Hellmann's
September 17 – Children's Hour
September 18 – Lady Next Door
September 20 – Lady Next Door
September 21 – Lady Next Door
September 21 – (audition)
September 22 – (audition)
September 24 – Children's Hour
September 24 – Main Street
September 24 – Miss Willie Bird
September 26 – Lady Next Door
September 27 – Lady Next Door
September 28 – Show Boat
September 30 – Lady Next Door
October 1 – Children's Hour
October 2 – Main Street
October 2 – Lady Next Door

October 3 – Buck Rogers (2 shows)
October 4 – Main Street
October 4 – Buck Rogers (2 shows)
October 5 – (audition)
October 5 – Buck Rogers (2 shows)
October 6 – Hellmann's
October 8 – Children's Hour
October 8 – Main Street
October 9 – Buck Rogers (2 shows)
October 10 – Buck Rogers (2 shows)
October 11 – Buck Rogers (2 shows)
October 11 – Main Street
October 12 – Buck Rogers (2 shows)
October 13 – Hellmann's
October 14 – Lady Next Door
October 15 – Children's Hour
October 15 – Big Ben
October 15 – Main Street
October 16 – Buck Rogers (2 shows)
October 16 – Lady Next Door
October 17 – American Legend
October 17 – Buck Rogers (2 shows)
October 18 – Buck Rogers (2 shows)
October 18 – Lady Next Door
October 18 – Main Street
October 19 – Buck Rogers (2 shows)
October 20 – Hellmann's
October 21 – Lady Next Door
October 22 – Children's Hour
October 22 – Main Street
October 23 – Buck Rogers (2 shows)
October 23 – Lady Next Door
October 24 – Buck Rogers (2 shows)
October 25 – Buck Rogers (2 shows)
October 25 – Main Street
October 26 – Buck Rogers (2 shows)
October 26 – Lady Next Door
October 26 – Hellmann's
October 28 – Lady Next Door
October 29 – Children's Hour
October 29 – Gilbert's
October 29 – Main Street
November 1 – Main Street
November 2 – (audition)
November 3 – (audition)
November 5 – Children's Hour
November 5 – Big Ben
November 5 – Main Street
November 6 – Buck Rogers (2 shows)
November 6 – Lady Next Door

November 7 – Buck Rogers (2 shows)
November 8 – Lady Next Door
November 8 – Buck Rogers (2 shows)
November 8 – Main Street
November 9 – Buck Rogers (2 shows)
November 10 – Hellmann's
November 12 – Children's Hour
November 12 – Gilbert's
November 12 – Main Street
November 15 – The Wizard of Oz
November 17 – Lady Next Door
November 18 – Lady Next Door
November 19 – Children's Hour
November 19 – Gilbert's
November 19 – Main Street
November 20 – The Wizard of Oz
November 21 – Eno
November 22 – The Wizard of Oz
November 22 – (audition)
November 23 – (audition)
November 24 – The Wizard of Oz
November 25 – Lady Next Door
November 26 – Children's Hour
November 26 – Gilbert's
November 26 – Main Street
November 27 – Lady Next Door
November 27 – The Wizard of Oz
November 29 – The Wizard of Oz
November 29 – Main Street
November 29 – Louise M. Olcott [Louisa
    May Alcott]
November 30 – Lady Next Door
December 1 – The Wizard of Oz
December 2 – Records
December 2 – Lady Next Door
December 3 – Children's Hour
December 3 – Gilberts
December 3 – Main Street
December 4 – The Wizard of Oz
December 4 – Lady Next Door
December 6 – Lady Next Door
December 6 – Main Street
December 7 – Wheatenaville
December 8 – Records
December 9 – Lady Next Door
December 10 – Children's Hour
December 10 – Gilberts
December 10 – Main Street
December 11 – Lady Next Door
December 11 – Gilberts

December 13 – Main Street
December 14 – Easy Aces
December 14 – Records
December 14 – Gilberts
December 15 – Easy Aces
December 15 – Wheatenaville
December 16 – Gilberts
December 16 – Lady Next Door
December 17 – Children's Hour
December 17 – Main Street
December 19 – Easy Aces
December 19 – Lady Next Door
December 20 – Easy Aces
December 20 – Lady Next Door
December 20 – Main Street
December 21 – Easy Aces
December 21 – Underwood
December 22 – Easy Aces
December 23 – Helen & Mary
December 24 – Children's Hour
December 24 – Bar X [Bobby Benson's Adventures]
December 24 – Col. Drama Guild
December 25 – Pragant of Christ [Pageant of Christ]
December 26 – Buck Rogers (2)
December 30 – Helen & Mary
December 30 – Lady Next Door
December 31 – Children's Hour

1934

January 3 – Lady Next Door
January 3 – Wheatenaville
January 4 – Fred Allen
January 6 – Motor Dame
January 6 – Major Andrews
January 7 – Children's Hour
January 7 – Bar X
January 9 – Tattered Man
January 10 – Lady Next Door
January 10 – Castoria
January 12 – Lady Next Door
January 13 – Lady Next Door
January 14 – Children's Hour
January 14 – Bar X
January 14 – Cream of Wheat
January 16 – Tattered Man
January 17 – Lady Next Door

January 18 – Wheatenaville
January 20 – Lady Next Door
January 21 – Children's Hour
January 21 – Bar X
January 21 – Hall of Fame
January 22 – Lady Next Door
January 23 – Buck Rogers (2)
January 24 – Buck Rogers (2)
January 25 – Buck Rogers (2)
January 26 – Lady Next Door
January 28 – Children's Hour
January 28 – Jack Benny (2)
January 29 – Buck Rogers (2)
January 30 – Tattered Man
February 1 – Lady Next Door
February 3 – Helen & Mary
February 4 – Children's Hour
February 4 – Cream of Wheat
February 5 – Lady Next Door
February 5 – Big Show
February 7 – Lady Next Door
February 7 – Dickens Pregent [Pageant]
February 8 – Lady Next Door
February 9 – (St. Georges Soc.)
February 11 – Children's Hour
February 11 – Big Ben
February 11 – Irene Rich [Irene Rich Dramas]
February 12 – American School of the Air
February 12 – Buck Rogers (2 shows)
February 13 – Lady Next Door
February 13 – Buck Rogers (2 shows)
February 14 – Buck Rogers (2 shows)
February 15 – Lady Next Door
February 16 – Maud Adams
February 18 – Children's Hour
February 22 – Winnie the Pooh
February 22 – Wheatenaville
February 22 – Show Boat
February 23 – Maud Adams
February 24 – Records
February 25 – Children's Hour
February 26 – (Records)
February 26 – Lady Next Door
February 27 – Tattered Man
February 28 – Conoco
March 1 – Lady Next Door
March 1 – Winnie the Pooh
March 2 – Maud Adams
March 3 – Helen & Mary

March 3 – Lady Next Door
March 3 – Ripley's
March 4 – Children's Hour
March 5 – Lady Next Door
March 6 – Lady Next Door
March 6 – Tattered Man
March 6 – (audition)
March 7 – (audition)
March 8 – Lady Next Door
March 10 – Helen & Mary
March 11 – Children's Hour
March 12 – Lady Next Door
March 13 – Lady Next Door
March 13 – Tattered Man
March 14 – Fred Allen (2)
March 15 – Show Boat (2)
March 17 – Helen & Mary
March 18 – Children's Hour
March 19 – Soconyland
March 20 – Lady Next Door
March 22 – Ford
March 24 – Helen & Mary
March 25 – Children's Hour
March 26 – Minnevitch
March 29 – Lady Next Door
March 31 – Helen & Mary
March 31 – Fox Col.
April 1 – Bar X
April 2 – Lady Next Door
April 3 – Minnevitch
April 4 – Wheatenaville
April 4 – (Lady MacKenzie)
April 5 – Lady Next Door
April 5 – Show Boat (2)
April 7 – (audition)
April 8 – Children's Hour
April 9 – Lady Next Door
April 9 – Big Show
April 10 – Minnevitch [P.A. with Borah
    Minnevich & His Harmonica
    Rascals]
April 10 – Camel's
April 11 – Lady Next Door
April 11 – Castoria
April 14 – Helen & Mary
April 14 – Bard of Erin
April 14 – Lady Next Door
April 15 – Children's Hour
April 17 – Lady Next Door
April 18 – Fred Allen (2)

April 19 – Lady Next Door
April 20 – (audition)
April 21 – Helen & Mary
April 21 – Lady Next Door
April 22 – Children's Hour
April 22 – Cream of Wheat
April 25 – Lady Next Door
April 25 – Cuckoo [The Cuckoo Hour]
April 26 – Ford
April 28 – Helen & Mary
April 28 – Lady Next Door
April 29 – Cream of Wheat
April 30 – Lady Next Door
April 30 – (audition)
May 3 – Buck Rogers (2)
May 5 – Helen & Mary
May 6 – Children's Hour
May 6 – Freddy Rich
May 7 – Lady Next Door
May 7 – Buck Rogers (2)
May 7 – Radio Guild
May 8 – Buck Rogers (2)
May 9 – Cuckoo
May 10 – Lady Next Door
May 12 – Helen & Mary
May 13 – Children's Hour
May 13 – Rose & Drums [Civil War
    stories]
May 14 – Buck Rogers (2)
May 14 – Tasty Yeast
May 15 – Buck Rogers (2)
May 16 – Lady Next Door
May 16 – Buck Rogers (2)
May 17 – Lady Next Door
May 19 – Let's Pretend
May 19 – Lady Next Door
May 20 – Children's Hour
May 21 – Buck Rogers (2)
May 22 – Buck Rogers (2)
May 23 – Buck Rogers (2)
May 26 – Let's Pretend
May 27 – Children's Hour
May 27 – 45 Min. Hollywood [45
    Minutes from Hollywood]
May 28 – Buck Rogers (2)
May 29 – Buck Rogers (2)
May 29 – Lady Next Door
May 30 – Buck Rogers (2)
May 31 – Buck Rogers (2)
June 1 – Al. Orchester

June 2 – Let's Pretend
June 2 – Lady Next Door
June 3 – Children's Hour
June 3 – 45 Min. Hollywood
June 4 – Buck Rogers (2)
June 4 – Lady Next Door
June 4 – (audition)
June 5 – Buck Rogers (2)
June 6 – Buck Rogers (2)
June 7 – Buck Rogers (2)
June 9 – Let's Pretend
June 10 – Children's Hour
June 12 – Buck Rogers (2)
June 13 – Buck Rogers (2)
June 14 – Buck Rogers (2)
June 14 – Show Boat (2)
June 15 – Certo
June 16 – Let's Pretend
June 16 – Lady Next Door
June 16 – (Abam & Strass) [Abraham
    & Strauss was large New York
    department store]
June 17 – Children's Hour
June 18 – Buck Rogers (2)
June 19 – Buck Rogers (2)
June 20 – Buck Rogers (2)
June 20 – Fred Allen (2)
June 21 – Show Boat (2)
June 23 – Let's Pretend
June 24 – Children's Hour
June 26 – Tasty Yeast
June 27 – Fred Allen (2)
June 28 – Winnie the Pooh
June 28 – Show Boat (2)
June 29 – Ai. of Orch.
August 18 – Lady Next Door
August 19 – Children's Hour
August 22 – Fred Allen (2)
August 25 – Let's Pretend
August 25 – Lady Next Door
August 26 – Children's Hour
August 28 – Lady Next Door
August 29 – Lady Next Door
August 29 – Fred Allen (2)
August 30 – Bar X
September 1 – Let's Pretend
September 1 – Lady Next Door
September 2 – Children's Hour
September 8 – Let's Pretend
September 8 – Lady Next Door

September 9 – Children's Hour
September 12 – Fred Allen (2)
September 12 – Fred Allen Com.
September 13 – (audition)
September 13 – Wheatenaville
September 14 – Lady Next Door
September 14 – (audition)
September 15 – Let's Pretend
September 16 – Children's Hour
September 17 – Lady Next Door
September 18 – Buck Rogers (2)
September 19 – Buck Rogers (2)
September 19 – Fred Allen (2)
September 19 – Fred Allen Com. (2)
September 20 – Buck Rogers (2)
September 20 – Wheatenaville
September 21 – True Story (2)
September 22 – Let's Pretend
September 23 – Children's Hour
September 24 – Buck Rogers
September 24 – Wheatenaville
September 25 – Buck Rogers (2)
September 25 – (audition)
September 26 – While Owl
September 29 – Let's Pretend
September 30 – Children's Hour
October 1 – Big Show
October 3 – (audition)
October 5 – Records
October 6 – True Story (2)
October 7 – Children's Hour
October 7 – Vicks
October 7 – Joe Penner
October 9 – Records
October 9 – Eno
October 9 – Lady Next Door
October 10 – Lady Next Door
October 10 – Eno
October 11 – Steel
October 13 – Let's Pretend
October 14 – Children's Hour
October 14 – Jack Benny (2)
October 15 – Buck Rogers (2)
October 16 – Buck Rogers (2)
October 17 – Buck Rogers (2)
October 17 – Fred Allen (2)
October 18 – Buck Rogers (2)
October 18 – Wheatenaville
October 19 – Gilberts (Thrills of
    Tomorrow premiere)

October 20 – Let's Pretend
October 20 – Romberg
October 21 – Children's Hour
October 23 – Palmoliver
October 24 – Fred Allen (2)
October 24 – American School of the Air
October 25 – Liberty
October 25 – Buck Rogers (2)
October 26 – Gilberts
October 26 – March of Time
October 27 – Let's Pretend
October 27 – Lady Next Door
October 29 – Buck Rogers (2)
October 30 – Records
October 31 – American School of the Air
October 31 – Wheatenaville
November 2 – Gilberts
November 3 – Let's Pretend
November 3 – Lady Next Door
November 4 – Children's Hour
November 5 – Wheatenaville
November 7 – American School of the Air
November 7 – Fred Allen (2)
November 8 – 45 Min. Hollywood
November 9 – Gilberts
November 10 – Let's Pretend
November 11 – Children's our
November 11 – Vicks
November 12 – Martins
November 13 – Buck Rogers (2)
November 13 – Records
November 14 – Buck Rogers (2)
November 14 – American School of the Air
November 14 – Fred Allen (2)
November 14 – Fred Allen Com. (2)
November 15 – Lady Next Door
November 16 – Gilberts
November 17 – Let's Pretend
November 17 – Lady Next Door
November 17 – Roxy [The Roxy Revue]
November 17 – (Naval Lodge Mason)
November 18 – Children's Hour
November 18 – Heart Thobs [Heart
    Throbs of the Hills]
November 19 – Buck Rogers (2)
November 20 – Buck Rogers (2)
November 21 – American School of the Air
November 22 – (audition)
November 22 – Lady Next Door
November 23 – Gilberts

November 24 – Let's Pretend
November 24 – Lady Next Door
November 25 – Children's Hour
November 26 – Lady Next Door
November 27 – American School of the Air
November 28 – American School of the Air
November 30 – Gilberts
December 1 – Let's Pretend
December 1 – Romberg
December 2 – Children's Hour
December 4 – Geo. Givot [Variety show]
December 5 – American School of the Air
December 6 – Show Boat
December 7 – Gilberts
December 8 – Let's Pretend
December 8 – Lady Next Door
December 9 – Children's Hour
December 9 – Vicks
December 9 – Jack Benny (2)
December 12 – American School of the Air
December 12 – Fred Allen (2)
December 14 – American School of the Air
December 14 – Gilberts
December 15 – Let's Pretend
December 15 – Lady Next Door
December 16 – Children's Hour
December 17 – (audition)
December 19 – American School of the Air
December 19 – Fred Allen (2)
December 22 – Let's Pretend
December 22 – Romberg
December 23 – Children's Hour
December 23 – Vicks
December 23 – Jack Benny (2)
December 23 – Walter Winchell (2)
    [Walter Winchell's Jergens Journal]
December 25 – Palmoliver
December 27 – 45 Min. Hollywood
December 29 – Let's Pretend
December 29 – Lady Next Door
December 30 – Children's Hour
December 31 – Records

1935

January 2 – Buck Rogers (2)
January 3 – Wheatenaville
January 3 – Fords
January 5 – Let's Pretend

January 5 – Lady Next Door
January 6 – Children's Hour
January 6 – Vicks
January 7-9 – (auditions)
January 10 – Lady Next Door
January 12 – Let's Pretend
January 13 – Children's Hour
January 14 – Lady Next Door
January 15 – Dark Enchantment
January 16 – American School of the Air
January 16 – Records
January 17 – Records
January 18 – Lady Next Door
January 19 – Let's Pretend
January 20 – Children's Hour
January 21 – Lady Next Door
January 22 – Dark Enchantment
January 23 – American School of the Air
January 23 – Fred Allen (2)
January 23 – Lady Next Door
January 24 – Lady Next Door
January 24 – Liberty
January 26 – Let's Pretend
January 27 – Joe Penner
January 27 – Children's Hour
January 29 – Lady Next Door
January 30 – American School of the Air
February 2 – Let's Pretend
February 3 – Children's Hour
February 6 – American School of the Air
February 6 – Lady Next Door
February 9 – Let's Pretend
February 9 – Roxy
February 10 – Children's Hour
February 11 – Lady Next Door
February 13 – American School of the Air
February 13 – Lady Next Door
February 15 – March of Time
February 16 – Let's Pretend
February 16 – Mickey of the Circus
February 17 – Children's Hour
February 17 – Eddie Cantor
February 19 – Lady Next Door
February 20 – American School of the Air
February 20 – Fred Allen (2)
February 22 – Wheatenaville
February 23 – Let's Pretend
February 24 – Children's Hour
February 26 – Lady Next Door
February 26 – Bobbie Benson

February 27 – American School of the Air
February 27 – Fred Allen (2)
February 28 – Bobbie Benson
March 1 – American School of the Air
March 1 – Bobbie Benson
March 2 – Let's Pretend
March 3 – Lady Next Door
March 3 – Children's Hour
March 4 – Bobbie Benson
March 5 – Lady Next Door
March 5 – Bobbie Benson
March 6 – American School of the Air
March 6 – Bobbie Benson
March 6 – Fred Allen (2)
March 7 – Housekeeping
March 7 – Bobbie Benson
March 7 – Show Boat
March 8 – Bobbie Benson
March 9 – Let's Pretend
March 10 – Children's Hour
March 11 – Bobbie Benson
March 12 – (audition)
March 12 – Bobbie Benson
March 13 – American School of the Air
March 13 – Bobbie Benson
March 14 – (Astoria Church) [P.A.
    Astoria Presbyterian Church in NY]
March 15 – Bobbie Benson
March 16 – Let's Pretend
March 17 – Children's Hour
March 17 – Joe Penner [The Baker's
    Broadcast]
March 18 – Bobbie Benson
March 19 – Lady Next Door
March 19 – Bobbie Benson
March 19 – (audition)
March 20 – Bobbie Benson
March 20 – American School of the Air
March 21 – Bobbie Benson
March 21 – Show Boat
March 22 – Bobbie Benson
March 23 – Let's Pretend
March 23 – Lady Next Door
March 24 – Children's Hour
March 24 – Man. Merry Go Round
    [Manhattan Merry-Go-Round]
March 25 – Bobbie Benson
March 26 – Lady Next Door
March 26 – Records
March 27 – American School of the Air

March 28 – Show Boat
March 30 – Let's Pretend
March 30 – Lady Next Door
March 31 – Children's Hour
March 31 – Lux
March 31 – Man. Merry Go Round
April 1 – Records
April 1 – Bobbie Benson
April 2 – Records
April 2 – Bobbie Benson
April 2 – Lady Next Door
April 3 – American School of the Air
April 3 – Fred Allen (2)
April 5 – (Prof. School)
April 5 – Bobbie Benson
April 6 – Let's Pretend
April 6 – Lady Next Door
April 7 – Children's Hour
April 8 – Bobbie Benson
April 8 – Records
April 9 – Records
April 9 – Bobbie Benson
April 10 – American School of the Air
April 10 – Bobbie Benson
April 11 – Bobbie Benson
April 12 – Bobbie Benson
April 13 – Let's Pretend
April 13 – Lady Next Door
April 14 – Children's Hour
April 15 – Records
April 15 – Bobbie Benson
April 16 – Records
April 16 – Lady Next Door
April 17 – American School of the Air
April 17 – Bobbie Benson
April 17 – Buck Rogers (2)
April 18 – Bobbie Benson
April 18 – Buck Rogers (2)
April 19 – Bobbie Benson
April 20 – Records
April 20 – Lady Next Door
April 21 – Children's Hour
April 22 – Records
April 22 – Buck Rogers (2)
April 22 – Bobbie Benson
April 23 – Buck Rogers (2)
April 23 – Records
April 23 – Lady Next Door
April 25 – Bobbie Benson
April 26 – Bobbie Benson

April 27 – Let's Pretend
April 27 – Lady Next Door
April 27 – (audition)
April 27 – Socony [Snow Village Sketches]
April 28 – Children's Hour
April 29 – Records
April 29 – Bobbie Benson
April 30 – Records
April 30 – (audition)
May 1 – American School of the Air
May 1 – Bobbie Benson
May 1 – Fred Allen (2)
May 2 – Bobbie Benson
May 3 – Bobbie Benson
May 4 – Let's Pretend
May 4 – Lady Next Door
May 5 – Children's Hour
May 6 – Bobbie Benson
May 7 – Bobbie Benson
May 7 – Lady Next Door
May 7 – (audition)
May 8 – American School of the Air
May 8 – Bobbie Benson
May 8 – Fred Allen (2)
May 9 – (audition)
May 11 – Let's Pretend
May 11 – Lady Next Door
May 12 – Children's Hour
May 16 – (Christ Church)
May 17 – (audition)
May 18 – Lady Next Door
May 18 – Records
May 19 – Children's Hour
May 19 – Joe Penner
May 20 – Buck Rogers (2)
May 20 – Bobbie Benson
May 21 – Records
May 21 – Buck Rogers (2)
May 21 – Bobbie Benson
May 22 – Buck Rogers (2)
May 23 – Buck Rogers (2)
May 23 – Records
May 25 – Let's Pretend
May 25 – Lady Next Door
May 26 – Children's Hour
May 27 – Buck Rogers (2)
May 29 – Buck Rogers (2)
May 30 – Buck Rogers (2)
May 31 – Bobbie Benson
June 1 – Let's Pretend

June 2 – Children's Hour
June 2 – Joe Penner
June 3 – Buck Rogers (2)
June 5 – Buck Rogers (2)
June 5 – Fred Allen (2)
June 6 – Buck Rogers (2)
June 8 – Let's Pretend
June 9 – Children's Hour
June 10 – Buck Rogers (2)
June 11 – Buck Rogers (2)
June 12 – Buck Rogers (2)
June 13 – Buck Rogers (2)
June 14 – (audition)
June 15 – Let's Pretend
June 15 – (Ridgefield Pk. Pol)
June 16 – Children's Hour
June 17 – Buck Rogers (2)
June 18 – Buck Rogers (2)
June 19 – Buck Rogers (2)
June 20 – (audition)
June 20 – Buck Rogers (2)
June 22 – Let's Pretend
June 22 – (U.S. Amb. Assn.)
June 22 – Lady Next Door
June 23 – Children's Hour
June 24 – Buck Rogers (2)
June 25 – Buck Rogers (2)
June 26 – Buck Rogers (2)
June 27 – Buck Rogers (2)
June 29 – Atlantic City
June 30 – Joe Penner
July 1 – Buck Rogers (2)
July 1 – (audition)
July 2 – Simpson Boys [Simpson Boys of
    Sprucehead Bay]
July 2 – Buck Rogers
July 3 – Buck Rogers
July 3 – Simpson Boys
July 5 – Records
July 5 – Winnie the Pooh
July 6 – Let's Pretend
July 6 – Lady Next Door
July 7 – Children's Hour
July 7 – Star Dust [Variety program]
July 9 – (audition)
July 9 – Winnie the Pooh
July 10 – Simpson Boys
July 13 – Let's Pretend
July 13 – Lady Next Door
July 14 – Children's Hour

July 15 – Buck Rogers (2)
July 16 – Simpson Boys
July 16 – Buck Rogers (2)
July 17 – Simpson Boys
July 17 – Buck Rogers (2)
July 18 – Better Housing
July 18 – (audition)
July 18 – Buck Rogers (2)
July 20 – Lady Next Door
July 21 – Children's Hour
July 22 – Alice Orchestila
July 23 – Winnie the Pooh
July 24 – (audition)
July 24 – (audition)
July 24 – Buck Rogers (2)
July 25 – MacBeth
July 25 – Buck Rogers (2)
July 27 – Simpson Boys
July 28 – Children's Hour
July 29 – Buck Rogers
July 30 – Simpson Boys
July 30 – Winnie the Pooh
July 31 – Simpson Boys
August 1 – Simpson Boys
August 1 – Winnie the Pooh
August 1 – Show Boat
August 3 – Let's Pretend
August 6 – Simpson Boys
August 6 – Records
August 7 – (Records)
August 10 – Let's Pretend
August 10 – Lady Next Door
August 12 – Lambardo Roard [Possibly
    on the road with Guy Lombardo]
August 13 – Simpson Boys
August 14 – Kate Smith
August 14 – (audition)
August 16 – (audition)
August 17 – Let's Pretend
August 18 – Children's Hour
August 22 – Simpson Boys
August 22 – Lady Next Door
August 23 – Simpson Boys
August 24 – Let's Pretend
August 24 – Lady Next Door
August 25 – Children's Hour
August 25 – Ray Perkins
August 27 – Records
August 27 – Records
August 31 – Let's Pretend

August 31 – Lady Next Door
September 2 – Lambardo Road
September 3 – Lady Next Door
September 3 – March of Time
September 5-7 – (Worchester, Mass.)
September 10 – (audition)
September 12 – Show Boat
September 13 – March of Time
September 13 – (audition)
September 14 – Let's Pretend
September 14 – Lady Next Door
September 15 – Children's Hour
September 16 – (audition)
September 18 – (audition)
September 19 – Show Boat
September 20 – March of Time
September 21 – Let's Pretend
September 22 – Children's Hour
September 22 – Lady Next Door
September 23 – (audition)
September 25 – (audition)
September 26 – Show Boat
September 28 – Let's Pretend
September 29 – Children's Hour
September 30 – Lambardo Road
September 30 – Lux
October 1 – (audition)
October 2 – March of Time
October 3 – Show Boat
October 5 – Let's Pretend
October 5 – Simpson Boys
October 6 – Children's Hour
October 8 – Simpson Boys
October 8 – Helen Hayes (2)
October 9 – Simpson Boys
October 10 – Show Boat
October 11 – Simpson Boys
October 12 – Let's Pretend
October 13 – Children's Hour
October 15 – Helen Hayes (2)
October 16 – Simpson Boys
October 16 – (audition)
October 17 – Simpson Boys
October 18 – Simpson Boys
October 19 – Let's Pretend
October 20 – Children's Hour
October 22 – Simpson Boys
October 22 – American School of the Air
October 22 – Buck Rogers (2)
October 22 – Helen Hayes (2)

October 23 – Simpson Boys
October 23 – American School of the Air
October 24 – Simpson Boys
October 23 – Cavalcade [Cavalcade
of America "The Spirit of
Competition"]
October 25 – Simpson Boys
October 26 – Let's Pretend
October 26 – Simpson Boys
October 26 – Lady Next Door
October 27 – Children's Hour
October 28 – Buck Rogers (2)
October 28 – Lambardo Road
October 28 – Andrew Carnegie
October 29 – Buck Rogers (2)
October 29 – Helen Hayes (2)
October 30 – American School of the Air
October 30 – Buck Rogers (2)
October 30 – Bobbie Benson
October 30 – Fred Allen (2)
October 31 – Buck Rogers (2)
November 1 – Bobbie Benson
November 1 – Pamoliver
November 2 – Let's Pretend
November 4 – Bobbie Benson
November 4 – Lambardo Road
November 5 – Helen Hayes (2)
November 6 – Simpson Boys
November 6 – American School of the Air
November 6 – Bobbie Benson
November 7 – Buck Rogers (2)
November 8 – Bobbie Benson
November 9 – Let's Pretend
November 10 – Children's Hour
November 11 – Buck Rogers (2)
November 11 – Bobbie Benson
November 11 – Lambardo Road
November 11 – Andrew Carnegie
November 12 – Simpson Boys
November 12 – American School of the Air
November 12 – Buck Rogers (2)
November 12 – Helen Hayes (2)
November 13 – American School of the Air
November 13 – Buck Rogers (2)
November 13 – Bobbie Benson
November 14 – Buck Rogers (2)
November 14 – March of Time
November 15 – Bobbie Benson
November 16 – Let's Pretend
November 16 – Lady Next Door

November 17 – Children's Hour
November 17 – (Quality Street)
November 18 – Bobbie Benson
November 19 – Helen Hayes (2)
November 20 – American School of the Air
November 22 – Bobbie Benson
November 23 – Let's Pretend
November 24 – Children's Hour
November 25 – Bobbie Benson
November 27 – American School of the Air
November 27 – Bobbie Benson
November 27 – Fred Allen (2)
November 29 – Bobbie Benson
November 29 – March of Time
November 30 – Let's Pretend
November 30 – Mark Twain
December 1 – Children's Hour
December 1 – Funnies
December 2 – Bobbie Benson
December 2 – (audition)
December 2 – March of Time
December 3 – March of Time
December 4 – American School of the Air
December 4 – Bobbie Benson
December 5 – Home Town
December 5 – Show Boat
December 6 – Simpson Boys
December 6 – Bobbie Benson
December 8 – Children's Hour
December 8 – Funnies
December 9 – Bobbie Benson
December 10 – Helen Hayes
December 11 – American School of the Air
December 11 – Bobbie Benson
December 11 – Buck Rogers (2)
December 12 – Show Boat
December 12 – Buck Rogers (2)
December 13 – Bobbie Benson
December 14 – Let's Pretend
December 14 – Lady Next Door
December 15 – Children's Hour
December 15 – Funnies
December 15 – Terhune (2)
December 16 – Bobbie Benson
December 16 – Buck Rogers (2)
December 17 – Buck Rogers (2)
December 18 – American School of the Air
December 18 – Bobbie Benson
December 18 – Fred Allen (2)
December 18 – Ipana (2)

December 19 – (audition)
December 19 – Show Boat
December 20 – Bobbie Benson
December 20 – Eternal Question
December 21 – Let's Pretend
December 22 – Children's Hour
December 22 – Funnies
December 23 – Bobbie Benson
December 24 – Simpson Boys
December 24 – Helen Hayes (2)
December 24 – Visit of St. Nick
December 25 – Bobbie Benson
December 25 – Cavalcade [Cavalcade
    of America "The Juvenile Court
    Story"]
December 25 – Fred Allen (2)
December 25 – Ipana (2)
December 26 – Simpson Boys
December 27 – Bobbie Benson
December 28 – Let's Pretend
December 28 – Lady Next Door
December 29 – Children's Hour
December 29 – Funnies
December 30 – Bobbie Benson
December 31 – Helen Hayes (2)

1936

January 1 – Col. Drama Guild
January 1 – Bobbie Benson
January 2 – March of Time
January 3 – Bobbie Benson
January 4 – Let's Pretend
January 5 – Children's Hour
January 5 – Funnies
January 5 – Echoes of New York
January 6 – Bobbie Benson
January 8 – Bobbie Benson
January 8 – American School of the Air
January 8 – March of Time
January 9 – Show Boat
January 10 – Bobbie Benson
January 11 – Let's Pretend
January 12 – Children's Hour
January 12 – Funnies
January 13 – Bobbie Benson
January 14 – Helen Hayes (2) ["The New
    Penny"]
January 14 – (audition)

January 15 – American School of the Air
January 15 – Bobbie Benson
January 15 – Fred Allen (2)
January 16 – Show Boat
January 17 – Bobbie Benson
January 18 – Let's Pretend
January 19 – Children's Hour
January 19 – Funnies
January 20 – Bobbie Benson
January 20 – (audition)
January 20 – (audition)
January 20 – Col. Drama Guild
January 22 – American School of the Air
January 22 – Bobbie Benson
January 23 – Show Boat
January 24 – Buck Rogers (2)
January 24 – Bobbie Benson
January 25 – Let's Pretend
January 26 – Children's Hour
January 26 – Funnies
January 27 – Buck Rogers (2)
January 27 – Bobbie Benson
January 29 – American School of the Air
January 29 – Buck Rogers (2)
January 29 – Bobbie Benson
January 29 – Fred Allen (2)
January 30 – News of Youth
January 30 – Show Boat
January 31 – Buck Rogers (2)
January 31 – Bobbie Benson
February 1 – Let's Pretend
February 2 – Children's Hour
February 2 – Funnies
February 2 – Eddie Cantor
February 3 – Buck Rogers (2)
February 3 – Bobbie Benson
February 4 – News of Youth
February 5 – Simpson Boys
February 5 – American School of the Air
February 5 – Buck Rogers (2)
February 5 – Bobbie Benson
February 6 – News of Youth
February 7 – Buck Rogers (2)
February 7 – Bobbie Benson
February 7 – March of Time
February 7 – (audition)
February 8 – Let's Pretend
February 8 – News of Youth
February 9 – Children's Hour
February 9 – Echoes of New York

February 10 – Bobbie Benson
February 10 – Buck Rogers (2)
February 11 – Records
February 12 – Buck Rogers (2)
February 12 – Bobbie Benson
February 14 – Buck Rogers (2)
February 14 – Bobbie Benson
February 15 – Let's Pretend
February 15 – Lady Next Door
February 15 – News of Youth
February 16 – Children's Hour
February 16 – Funnies
February 17 – Simpson Boys
February 17 – Bobbie Benson
February 18 – Helen Hayes (2)
February 19 – American School of the Air
February 19 – Bobbie Benson
February 19 – Fred Allen (2)
February 20 – News of Youth
February 21 – Bobbie Benson
February 25 – News of Youth
February 26 – American School of the Air
February 26 – Dreams of Long Ago (2)
February 27 – Show Boat
February 28 – Buck Rogers (2)
February 29 – Let's Pretend
February 29 – Records
February 29 – News of Youth
March 1 – Children's Hour
March 1 – Funnies
March 2 – Buck Rogers (2)
March 4 – American School of the Air
March 4 – Buck Rogers (2)
March 4 – Fred Allen (2)
March 5 – Show Boat
March 6 – Buck Rogers (2)
March 6 – March of Time
March 7 – Let's Pretend
March 7 – Palmolive (2)
March 8 – Echoes of New York
March 9 – Buck Rogers (2)
March 10 – Helen Hayes (2)
March 11 – American School of the Air
March 11 – Buck Rogers (2)
March 13 – Buck Rogers (2)
March 14 – Let's Pretend
March 15 – Children's Hour
March 15 – Funnies
March 18 – Simpson Boys
March 18 – American School of the Air

March 18 – Fred Allen (2)
March 19 – Show Boat
March 21 – Let's Pretend
March 22 – Children's Hour
March 22 – Funnies
March 22 – Echoes of New York
March 25 – American School of the Air
March 25 – March of Time
March 28 – Let's Pretend
March 29 – Children's Hour
March 29 – Funnies
April 1 – Fred Allen (2)
April 1 – American School of the Air
April 4 – Let's Pretend
April 5 – Children's Hour
April 5 – Funnies
April 8 – American School of the Air
April 8 – Fred Allen (2)
April 8 – March of Time
April 9 – Show Boat
April 11 – Let's Pretend
April 12 – Children's Hour
April 12 – Funnies
April 13 – Simpson Boys
April 15 – Fred Allen (2)
April 16 – Death Valley Days
April 18 – Let's Pretend
April 19 – Children's Hour
April 20 – Bobbie Benson
April 22 – American School of the Air
April 22 – Bobbie Benson
April 23 – News of Youth
April 24 – Bobbie Benson
April 25 – News of Youth
April 26 – Children's Hour
April 26 – Funnies
April 26 – Echoes of New York
April 26 – Paul Whiteman (2)
April 28 – News of Youth
April 29 – American School of the Air
April 29 – (audition)
May 1 – (Newburg, NY)
May 2 – (Newburg, NY)
May 3 – Children's Hour
May 3 – Paul Whiteman (2)
May 5 – News of Youth
May 7 – Show Boat (2)
May 9 – Let's Pretend
May 10 – Children's Hour
May 10 – Funnies

May 10 – Paul Whiteman (2)
May 12 – News of Youth
May 13 – Fred Allen (2)
May 14 – News of Youth
May 15 – Bobbie Benson
May 16 – Let's Pretend
May 16 – News of Youth
May 17 – Children's Hour
May 17 – Funnies
May 18 – (audition)
May 20 – (Lady MacKenzie)
May 21 – Death Valley Days
May 23 – Let's Pretend
May 23 – News of Youth
May 24 – Children's Hour
May 24 – Funnies
May 26 – News of Youth
May 26 – (audition)
May 27 – Cavalcade [Cavalcade of
    America "Resourcefulness"]
May 28 – Records
May 28 – News of Youth
May 30 – Let's Pretend
May 31 – Children's Hour
May 31 – Funnies
June 3 – (audition)
June 4 – Records
June 4 – News of Youth
June 5 – (christening of boat)
June 6 – Let's Pretend
June 6 – News of Youth
June 6 – (Peekskill) [P.A. in NY]
June 7 – Children's Hour
June 7 – Funnies
June 10 – Fred Allen (2)
June 10 – Ipana (2)
June 11 – Records
June 11 – News of Youth
June 13 – Let's Pretend
June 13 – News of Youth
June 14 – Children's Hour
June 20 – Let's Pretend
June 20 – News of Youth
June 21 – Children's Hour
June 21 – Funnies
June 24 – Gang Busters
June 27 – Let's Pretend
June 27 – News of Youth
June 28 – Children's Hour
June 28 – Funnies

July 1 – (audition)
July 2 – News of Youth
July 5 – Children's Hour
July 5 – Radio Album
July 6 – Bobbie Benson
July 7 – News of Youth
July 8 – Bobbie Benson
July 9 – News of Youth
July 9 – Death Valley Days
July 11 – Let's Pretend
July 12 – Children's Hour
July 12 – Funnies
July 14 – News of Youth
July 15 – Gang Busters
July 16 – News of Youth
July 17 – (audition)
July 18 – Let's Pretend
July 19 – Children's Hour
July 19 – Funnies
July 21 – (audition)
July 21 – News of Youth
July 23 – News of Youth
July 24 – (audition)
July 24 – (audition)
July 25 – News of Youth
July 25 – Let's Pretend
July 26 – Funnies
July 26 – Feen-A-Mint
July 27 – (audition, FoxyGr. PA)
July 28 – (audition, Hoople)
July 28 – (audition, Foxy)
July 28 – News of Youth
July 29 – Renfrew (2) [Renfrew of the
    Mounted Police – Tales of the
    Canadian Mounted Police]
July 29 – March of Time
July 30 – Renfrew (2)
July 31 – Renfrew (2)
August 1 – Let's Pretend
August 1 – News of Youth
August 2 – Children's Hour
August 2 – Funnies
August 3 – Renfrew (2)
August 4 – News of Youth
August 4 – Renfrew (2)
August 4 – March of Time
    [Documentary-type program]
August 5 – Old Dr. Jim [Probably daily
    soap opera]
August 5 – Renfrew (2)

August 6 – Renfrew (2)
August 6 – Death Valley Days
August 8 – Let's Pretend
August 10 – Old Dr. Jim
August 10 – (audition, McK. & Jor.)
August 11 – Old Dr. Jim
August 11 – News of Youth
August 12 – Cavalcade [Cavalcade of
    America "Concert Band Comes to
    Town"]
August 13 – News of Youth
August 14 – Old Dr. Jim
August 15 – Let's Pretend
August 15 – News of Youth
August 16 – Children's Hour
August 16 – Funnies
August 17 – (rehearsal, Phil. Lord)
August 18 – (rehearsal, Phil. Lord)
August 18 – News of Youth
August 20 – (audition, Phil. Lord)
August 20 – News of Youth
August 22 – News of Youth
August 23 – Children's Hour
August 23 – Funnies
August 24 – Home Sweet Home [Daily
    serial]
August 25 – News of Youth
August 26 – (audition, McK. & Jor.)
August 26 – Town Hall (2) [Town Hall
    Tonight with Fred Allen]
August 27 – Records
August 27 – News of Youth
August 28 – March of Time
August 30 – Children's Hour
August 30 – Funnies
September 8 – News of Youth
September 10 – News of Youth
September 12 – Let's Pretend
September 13 – Children's Hour
September 13 – Funnies
September 15 – News of Youth
September 16 – Gang Busters
September 19 – Let's Pretend
September 19 – News of Youth
September 20 – Children's Hour
September 20 – Funnies
September 21 – March of Time
September 22 – News of Youth
September 24 – News of Youth
September 26 – Let's Pretend

September 26 – Workshop
September 27 – Children's Hour
September 27 – Funnies
September 28 – Jack Masters [Treasure
    Adventures of Jack Masters]
September 29 – News of Youth
September 30 – Jack Masters
October 2 – Jack Masters
October 4 – Children's Hour
October 4 – Funnies
October 5 – Renfrew (2)
October 5 – Jack Masters
October 7 – Jack Masters
October 7 – Fred Allen (2)
October 8 – Kate Smith [Variety show
    with dramatic sequence]
October 9 – Jack Masters
October 10 – News of Youth
October 11 – Children's Hour
October 11 – Funnies
October 12 – Jack Masters
October 12 – Helen Hayes (2)
October 13 – News of Youth
October 14 – Jack Masters
October 14 – American School of the Air
October 15 – News of Youth
October 16 – Jack Masters
October 17 – News of Youth
October 18 – Children's Hour
October 18 – Funnies
October 18 – We the People ["Human
    interest" stories]
October 19 – Jack Masters
October 21 – American School of the Air
October 21 – Jack Masters
October 21 – Fred Allen (2)
October 22 – Kate Smith
October 23 – Jack Masters
October 24 – Let's Pretend
October 24 – News of Youth
October 25 – Children's Hour
October 25 – Funnies
October 26 – Jack Masters
October 27 – News of Youth
October 28 – Jack Masters
October 29 – News of Youth
October 30 – Jack Masters
October 30 – Welch [Irene Rich Dramas
    sponsored by Welch Grape Juice]
October 31 – Let's Pretend

October 31 – Barn Show
November 1 – Children's Hour
November 1 – Funnies
November 1 – Magic Key [Variety show
    AKA The Magic Key of RCA]
November 2 – Jack Masters
November 4 – American School of the Air
November 4 – Jack Masters
November 4 – Gang Busters
November 5 – March of Time
November 6 – Jack Masters
November 7 – Let's Pretend
November 8 – Children's Hour
November 8 – Funnies
November 9 – Jack Masters
November 11 – Fred Allen (2)
November 11 – Jack Masters
November 13 – Jack Masters
November 14 – Let's Pretend
November 15 – Funnies
November 16 – Jack Masters
November 18 – American School of the Air
November 18 – Jack Masters
November 18 – Renfrew (2)
November 19 – Renfrew (2)
November 20 – Jack Masters
November 20 – Renfrew (2)
November 20 – True Story (2)
November 22 – Children's Hour
November 23 – Jack Masters
November 25 – American School of the Air
November 25 – Easy Aces
November 25 – Jack Masters
November 26 – Kate Smith [Kate Smith
    A&P Bandwagon]
November 27 – Jack Masters
November 28 – Let's Pretend
November 28 – News of Youth
November 29 – Children's Hour
November 29 – Funnies
November 30 – Jack Masters
December 2 – American School of the Air
December 2 – Jack Masters
December 2 – Records (2)
December 3 – Billy & Betty [Children's
    show with Billy & Betty White]
December 3 – Kate Smith
December 4 – Jack Masters
December 4 – Billy & Betty
December 5 – Let's Pretend

December 5 – Barn Show
December 6 – Children's Hour
December 6 – Funnies
December 7 – Jack Masters
December 7 – Billy & Betty
December 8 – Billy & Betty
December 9 – American School of the Air
December 9 – Jack Masters
December 10 – Billy & Betty
December 11 – Jack Masters
December 11 – Billy & Betty
December 11 – (Clan MacKenzie)
December 12 – Let's Pretend
December 12 – Barn Show
December 13 – Children's Hour
December 13 – Capt. Diamond [Captain Diamond's Ads]
December 13 – Echoes of New York
December 14 – Jack Masters
December 14 – Billy & Betty
December 15 – Billy & Betty
December 16 – American School of the Air
December 16 – Billy & Betty
December 16 – Jack Masters
December 16 – Fred Allen (2)
December 17 – Billy & Betty
December 18 – Jack Masters
December 18 – Records
December 19 – Let's Pretend
December 19 – Thornton Fisher
December 20 – Funnies
December 20 – Children's Hour
December 21 – Jack Masters
December 21 – Helen Hayes New Penny (2) [Helen Hayes Theater "New Penny"]
December 23 – Jack Masters
December 23 – Fred Allen (2)
December 24 – Christmas Party [P.A.]
December 24 – Dicken's A Christmas Carol
December 25 – Jack Masters
December 25 – Toyland [Probably one-time Christmas show]
December 26 – Let's Pretend
December 26 – Barn Show
December 27 – Children's Hour
December 27 – Funnies
December 30 – Gang Busters
December 31 – March of Time

1937

January 1 – Col. Dram.
January 2 – Let's Pretend
January 3 – Children's Hour
January 3 – Funnies
January 4 – Billy & Betty
January 5 – Billy & Betty
January 6 – Billy & Betty
January 7 – Billy & Betty
January 7 – Bert Lahr
January 8 – Billy & Betty
January 9 – Let's Pretend
January 9 – Barn Show
January 10 – Children's Hour
January 10 – Funnies
January 11 – Billy & Betty
January 11 – Helen Hayes (2)
January 13 – American School of the Air
January 13 – Billy & Betty
January 14 – Floyd Gibbins [Colgate True Adventure]
January 15 – Billy & Betty
January 16 – Let's Pretend
January 17 – Children's Hour
January 17 – Funnies
January 20 – Fred Allen (2)
January 22 – Records
January 23 – Barn Show
January 23 – (Kearney, New Jersey)
January 24 – Children's Hour
January 24 – Funnies
January 24 – Capt. Diamond
January 24 – Echoes of New York
January 25 – Billy & Betty
January 26 – Billy & Betty
January 27 – American School of the Air
January 27 – Billy & Betty
January 27 – Fred Allen (2)
January 29 – Billy & Betty
January 30 – Let's Pretend
January 31 – Children's Hour
January 31 – Funnies
January 31 – Echoes of New York
February 1 – Warden Laws
February 3 – Billy & Betty
February 4 – Billy & Betty
February 5 – News of Youth
February 6 – Let's Pretend
February 6 – Shell Show

February 7 – Children's Hour
February 7 – Funnies
February 8 – (audition)
February 9 – (audition)
February 10 – American School of the Air
February 10 – News of Youth
February 12 – Singing Lady
February 13 – Let's Pretend
February 13 – Barn Show
February 13 – Joe Cook [Circus Night in
    Silvertown]
February 14 – Children's Hour
February 15 – (audition)
February 17 – American School of the Air
February 19 – (audition)
February 19 – News of Youth
February 20 – Let's Pretend
February 20 – Barn Show
February 20 – Joe Cook
February 21 – Children's Hour
February 21 – Funnies
February 22 – News of Youth
February 24 – American School of the Air
February 24 – News of Youth
February 24 – Fred Allen (2)
February 25 – Hy Brown [Probably
    an audition for writer/director/
    producer Hi Brown]
February 26 – News of Youth
February 27 – Let's Pretend
February 27 – Barn Show
February 28 – Children's Hour
February 28 – Funnies
March 1 – News of Youth
March 3 – American School of the Air
March 3 – News of Youth
March 3 – Fred Allen (2)
March 5 – News of Youth
March 6 – Let's Pretend
March 6 – Barn Show
March 6 – Joe Cook
March 8 – News of Youth
March 10 – American School of the Air
March 10 – News of Youth
March 12 – News of Youth
March 12 – Death Valley Days
March 13 – Let's Pretend
March 13 – Barn Show
March 14 – Children's Hour
March 14 – Funnies

March 15 – News of Youth
March 15 – Billy & Betty
March 16 – Billy & Betty
March 17 – American School of the Air
March 17 – News of Youth
March 19 – News of Youth
March 20 – Let's Pretend
March 20 – Barn Show
March 20 – Joe Cook
March 21 – Children's Hour
March 21 – Funnies
March 21 – Work Shop
March 22 – Billy & Betty
March 24 – American School of the Air
March 25 – Billy & Betty
March 26 – March of Time
March 27 – Let's Pretend
March 28 – Funnies
March 31 – Fred Allen (2)
April 2 – Radio Guild
April 3 – Let's Pretend
April 4 – Children's Hour
April 4 – Funnies
April 6 – Billy & Betty
April 7 – American School of the Air
April 7 – Billy & Betty
April 8 – Records
April 10 – Let's Pretend
April 10 – Barn Show
April 10 – Joe Cook
April 11 – Children's Hour
April 11 – Funnies
April 14 – American School of the Air
April 14 – Fred Allen (2)
April 15 – Records
April 16 – Geo. Rector
April 17 – Let's Pretend
April 17 – Barn Show
April 18 – Children's Hour
April 18 – Funnies
April 21 – American School of the Air
April 22 – Radio Music Hall
April 23 – David Harum [Daily soap opera]
April 24 – Let's Pretend
April 24 – Barn Show
April 25 – Children's Hour
April 25 – Funnies
April 26 – Ma & Pa [Serial drama]
April 27 – Ma & Pa
April 28 – David Harum

April 28 – American School of the Air
April 28 – Ma & Pa
April 29 – Records
April 29 – Ma & Pa
April 30 – David Harum
April 30 – Ma & Pa
May 1 – Let's Pretend
May 1 – Joe Cook
May 2 – Children's Hour
May 2 – Funnies
May 2 – Bert Lahr [Comedy/variety
    program]
May 3 – (audition)
May 3 – Ma & Pa
May 4 – Ma & Pa
May 5 – David Harum
May 5 – (audition)
May 5 – Ma & Pa
May 6 – Ma & Pa
May 7 – Records
May 7 – Ma & Pa
May 8 – Let's Pretend
May 8 – Snow Village [Sketches]
May 9 – Children's Hour
May 9 – Funnies
May 10 – Ma & Pa
May 11 – Ma & Pa
May 13 – Billy & Betty
May 13 – Floyd Gibbins
May 15 – Let's Pretend
May 15 – Barn Show
May 16 – Children's Hour
May 16 – Funnies
May 17 – Ma & Pa
May 18 – Billy & Betty
May 19 – Billy & Betty
May 20 – Geo. Rector
May 20 – Billy & Betty
May 22 – Let's Pretend
May 22 – Barn Show
May 22 – (Warners) [Possibly P.A. at one
    of the Warners theaters]
May 23 – Children's Hour
May 23 – Funnies
May 26 – Ma & Pa
May 26 – Fred Allen (2)
May 27 – Ma & Pa
May 28 – Records
May 28 – Ma & Pa
May 28 – Death Valley Days

May 29 – Let's Pretend
May 29 – Wyandote Players
May 30 – Children's Hour
May 31 – Billy & Betty
May 31 – Ma & Pa
June 2 – Gang Busters
June 4 – (audition)
June 5 – Let's Pretend
June 5 – Barn Show
June 6 – Children's Hour
June 6 – Echoes of New York
June 7 – Ma & Pa
June 8 – Billy & Betty
June 8 – Ma & Pa
June 9 – Peggy Wood
June 9 – Fred Allen (2)
June 11 – Billy & Betty
June 11 – Log Cabin R [The Jack Haley
    Show AKA Log Cabin Jamboree]
June 11 – King Tot R
June 11 – Aunt Mary R
June 12 – Let's Pretend
June 13 – Children's Hour
June 13 – Funnies
June 13 – Work Shop
June 15 – Billy & Betty
June 19 – Let's Pretend
June 19 – Barn Show
June 20 – Children's Hour
June 20 – Work Shop
June 20 – Sealtest
June 24 – Peter Pan
June 26 – Let's Pretend
June 26 – Barn Show
June 26 – (audition)
June 27 – Children's Hour
July 3 – Let's Pretend
July 3 – Barn Show
July 4 – Children's Hour
July 4 – Braves of Brave
July 4 – Sealtest
July 5 – Billy & Betty
July 6 – Billy & Betty
July 7 – Town Hall (2)
July 10 – Let's Pretend
July 10 – Barn Show
July 11 – Children's Hour
July 13 – Billy & Betty
July 15 – Log Cabin R
July 24 – Let's Pretend

July 24 – Barn Show
July 25 – Children's Hour
July 25 – Sealtest
July 28 – Town Hall (2)
July 29 – March of Time
August 1 – Sealtest
August 4 – Town Hall (2)
August 9 – Billy & Betty
August 10 – (audition)
August 11 – Town Hall (2)
August 16 – Log Cabin R
August 19 – March of Time
August 21 – Let's Pretend
August 22 – Sealtest
August 23 – Killy Kelly (2) [NBC soap
    opera Kitty Kelley]
August 25 – Town Hall (2)
August 28 – Let's Pretend
August 28 – Barn Show
August 29 – Children's Hour
August 29 – Dreams of Long Ago
September 1 – Town Hall (2)
September 1 – Commercial (2)
September 4 – Let's Pretend
September 4 – Barn Show
September 5 – Children's Hour
September 9 – March of Time
September 10 – Log Cabin R
September 11 – Let's Pretend
September 11 – Barn Show
September 12 – Children's Hour
September 12 – (off to Hollywood)
September 29 – Texaco (2)
October 5 – Packard (2) [Variety hour
    with Fred Astaire]

October 6 – Texaco
October 25 – Grape Nut (2)
October 25 – Commercial (2)
November 11 – Maxwell House (2)
November 17 – Town Hall (2)
November 18 – Maxwell House
November 16 – Packard (2)
November 24 – Fred Allen (2)
December 1 – Fred Allen (2)
December 7 – Packard (2)
December 8 – Fred Allen (2)
December 15 – Fred Allen (2)
December 21 – Big Town (2)
December 22 – Fred Allen (2)
December 29 – Fred Allen (2)
December 29 – Wops
December 30 – Wops

1938

January 5 – Wops
January 6 – Wops
January 22 – Jack Haley (2)
January 23 – Jean Hersholt [Dr. Christian]
January 28 – Texaco (2)
February 1 – Packard (2)
February 9 – Texaco (2)
February 14 – Texaco (2)
February 20 – Hollywood Playhouse (2)
March 1 – Big Town (2)
March 16 – Hollywood Parade
April 3 – The Mickey Mouse Theatre of
    the Air

(Here, the little black notebook ends.)

OTHER RADIO CREDITS

December 9, 1938 – Big Town
February 7, 1939 – Fibber McGee and
    Molly
February 21, 1939 – Fibber McGee and
    Molly
March 20, 1939 – Lux Radio Theatre ("It
    Happened One Night" with Clark
    Gable and Claudette Colbert)
June 11, 1939 – Radio Guild

March 17, 1940 – The Campbell Playhouse
October 15, 1940 – Fibber McGee and
    Molly
December 29, 1940 – Jack Benny
February 5, 1941 – It's Time to Smile
May 16, 1941 – The Great Gildersleeve
    (audition)
August 31, 1941 – March 21, 1957 – The
    Great Gildersleeve

Rehearsing *The Great Gildersleeve*.

October 20, 1941 – Lux Radio Theatre
("Blood and Sand" with Tyrone
Power and Annabella)
November 15, 1941 – NBC's Fifteenth
Anniversary Party
1942 – This Is My Best ("Around the World
in Eighty Days" with Orson Welles)
July 23, 1942 – Command Performance
(with Pat O'Brien, Francis
Langford, Alfred Newman & the
20th Century Fox Studio Orchestra,
Hal "Gildersleeve" Peary, Lillian
"Birdie" Randolph, Cab Calloway
Orchestra)
November 10, 1942 – The George Burns
and Gracie Allen Show
September 18, 1943 – Command
Performance – (with Ronald
Colman, Jascha Heifetz, Rise
Stevens, Lena Horne, Robert
Benchley, 43rd Army Air Forces
Band, Gardner Field Band)
February 18, 1943 – The Bob Burns Show
April 1, 1943 – The Bob Burns Show

April 8, 1943 – The Bob Burns Show
April 22, 1943 – The Bob Burns Show
May 2, 1943 – The Bob Burns Show
May 6, 1943 – The Bob Burns Show
May 20, 1943 – The Bob Burns Show
June 17, 1943 – The Bob Burns Show
December 2, 1943 – Suspense
February 23, 1944 Radio Almanac
March 1, 1944 – Radio Almanac
April 27, 1944 – Suspense
June 15, 1944 – The Dinah Shore
Program
June 15, 1944 – Birdseye Open House
(with Phil Harris)
November 16, 1944 – Suspense ("Dead of
the Night" with Robert Cummings)
November 21, 1944 – This Is My Best
February 8, 1945 – Suspense
April 18, 1945 – Mail Call
November 8, 1945 – Command
Performance
1945 – The Anderson Family
March 18, 1946 – The Harry Von Zell
Show (audition; with Frank Nelson)

August 8, 1946 – Suspense
September 29, 1946 –
June 18, 1954 – The Phil Harris/Alice
    Faye Show
October 14, 1946 – The Cavalcade of
    America
November 4, 1946 – The Cavalcade of
    America
November 12, 1946 – Fibber McGee and
    Molly
1947 – The Anderson Family (several)
February 14, 1947 – The Alan Young
    Show
March 9, 1947 – The Fitch Bandwagon
July 13, 1947 – The Jack Paar Show
July 24, 1947 – Family Theater ("Brass
    Buttons" with Maureen O'Hara,
    Regis Toomey)
October 21, 1947 – Here's To Veterans
January 8, 1948 – Family Theater ("The
    Happiest Person in the World" with
    William Bendix)
March 30, 1948 – Fibber McGee and
    Molly
April 10, 1948 – The Kid on the Corner
    (audition; with Sheldon Leonard)
April 25, 1948 – The Fitch Bandwagon
May 23, 1948 – Guest Star
December 25, 1948 – Command
    Performance (with Cass Daley,
    Jerry Colonna, Frank Nelson, Mel
    Blanc, Francis X. Bushman, Donald
    Crisp, William Conrad, Jeffrey
    Silver and Jane Webb)

October 26, 1950 – Suspense
March 22, 1951 – Screen Directors'
    Playhouse ("The Great Lover" with
    Bob Hope and Rhonda Fleming)
September 26, 1952 – Cascade of Stars
    (with Groucho Marx, Judy Canova,
    etc.)
June 2, 1953 – Fibber McGee and Molly
December 30, 1953 – Crime Classics
    ("Coyle and Richardson: Why They
    Hung In A Spanking Breeze")
January 6, 1954 – Crime Classics ("The
    Younger Brothers: Why Some Of
    Them Grew No Older")
April 13, 1954 – Fibber McGee and Molly
May 17, 1954 – Fibber McGee and Molly
January 13, 1958 – You Bet Your Life
    (promo spot for NBC)
February 13, 1972 – Same Time, Same
    Station (Rebroadcast of early
    shows)
November 26, 1973 – The Hollywood
    Radio Theatre
November 27, 1973 – The Hollywood
    Radio Theatre
November 28, 1973 – The Hollywood
    Radio Theatre
November 29, 1973 – The Hollywood
    Radio Theatre
November 30, 1973 – The Hollywood
    Radio Theatre

MISC. UNDATED RADIO APPEARANCES

Substituted for Johnny, the Philip Morris call boy
Mail Call (episode #141 with Hal Peary)

FILMS

1938 – Sally, Irene and Mary (20th
    Century-Fox)
1938 – A Trip to Paris (20th Century-Fox;
    The Jones Family series)
1938 – Lord Jeff (MGM)

1938 – Prairie Moon (Republic)
1939 – You Can't Cheat an Honest Man
    (Universal)
1939 – They Shall Have Music (United
    Artists)

A Yank at Eaton, MGM, 1942.

1939 – Tower of London (Universal)
1939 – The Spirit of Culver (Universal)
1939 – The Family Next Door (Universal)
1939 – Boy Slaves (RKO)
1940 – Emergency Squad (Paramount)
1940 – Framed (Universal)
1940 – Under Texas Skies (Republic)
1940 – The Villain Still Pursued Her (RKO)
1940 – Military Academy (Columbia)
1940 – Let's Make Music (RKO)
1941 – Ride, Kelly, Ride (20th Century-Fox)
1941 – The Haunted Mouse (Warner Brothers; cartoon)
1941 – Horror Island (Universal)
1941 – Out of the Fog (Warner Brothers)
1942 – Sing Your Worries Away (RKO)
1942 – Broadway (Universal)
1942 – Invisible Agent (Universal)
1942 – The Pride of the Yankees (RKO)
1942 – A Yank at Eaton (MGM)
1942 – Who Done It? (Universal)

1942 – Thunder Birds (20th Century-Fox)
1942 – Moonlight in Havana (Universal)
1942 – Gorilla Man (Warner Brothers)
1942 – Eyes in the Night (MGM)
1943 – Mystery Broadcast (Republic)
1943 – Fish Fry (Andy Panda cartoon)
1943 – Gildersleeve on Broadway (RKO)
1943 – The Painter and the Pointer (Universal; Andy Panda cartoon)
1944 – The Lodger (20th Century-Fox)
1944 – Her Primitive Man (Universal)
1944 – Pin-Up Girl (20th Century-Fox)
1944 – Follow the Boys (Universal)
1944 – Casanova Brown (RKO)
1944 – Bowery to Broadway (Universal)
1945 – I'll Remember April (Universal)
1945 – Molly and Me (20th Century-Fox)
1945 – It's in the Bag! (United Artists)
1945 – Crow Crazy (Universal; Andy Panda cartoon)
1946 – How Do You Do? (PRC)
1946 – Apple Andy (Universal; Andy Panda cartoon)

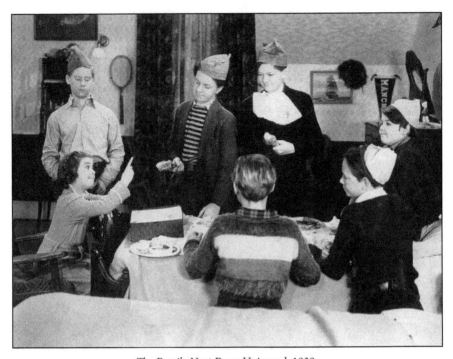

The Family Next Door, Universal, 1939.

1946 – Mousie Came Home (Universal;
   Andy Panda cartoon)
1946 – The Wacky Weed (Universal;
   Andy Panda cartoon)

1948 – The Playful Pelican (Universal;
   Andy Panda cartoon)
1949 – Scrappy Birthday (Universal;
   Andy Panda cartoon)

TELEVISION

1957 – The Woody Woodpecker Show (Andy Panda)
1961 – The Bullwinkle Show (Sherman)
1967 – George of the Jungle
1969 – The Dudley Do-Right Show

CPSIA information can be obtained
at www.ICGtesting.com
Printed in the USA
BVHW040225020421
604000BV00018B/411